KISSING THE TARMAC
Winning the War With PTSD

Kissing the Tarmac: Winning the War With PTSD

Copyright © 2016 by James Hansen

ISBN 978-0-692-75245-6

All rights reserved. No part of this book may be reproduced or transmitted in any form or by any means, electronic or mechanical, including photocopying, without the express written consent of the author, except where permitted by law.

Cover photo courtesy of *Washington Post*

Color photographs taken during the war were by the author with a Kodak Instamatic camera.

Book design by Stories To Tell, www.StoriesToTellBooks.com

KISSING THE TARMAC
Winning the War With PTSD

James Hansen

This memoir was written for my sons, Niles and Nathan, and my grandsons, Sam, Eli, and Tom. I have never shared anything about the Vietnam War with them until now.

I would like to dedicate this book to all those challenged by
PTSD,
no matter the cause.
Peace of mind is possible.

Charlie Company
March 1, 1968 — February 27, 1969

Killed In Action

Arambula, Paul	Bachileda, Bern	Barker, Kenneth
Barnum, Gary	Bennett, Joseph	Blanco, Heriberto
Boyett, Thomas	Brehn, Thomas	Brown, David
Cash, David	Collier, Timothy	Davis, Paul
Dorchak, George	Dunlap, Richard	Evans, Michael
Foster, James	Franklin, John	Frappiea, Fred
Friend, Richard	Gawel, Walter	Gomez, Jesus
Grant, William	Hayden, Troy	Heal, Henry
Holjes, Frederick	Jones, William	Kenney, Terry
Koch, James	Krause, Manfred	Lopez, Ramos
Martin, George	Mosley, Robert	Nicholson, George
Palmer, Millard	Pass, John	Peterson, Donald
Pressley, Cornelius	Ptak, Thomas	Purdue, Donald
Pyle, Charles	Robinson, Timothy	Santiago, Nelson
Saunders, Geoffrey	Sharrock, Edward	Smith, Raymond
Stone, George	Tackett, Ruben	White, Terry
Williams, Richard		

Contents

The Little Red Notebook	ix
The Letters	xi
So This is Combat	1
The Morning	1
The Afternoon	7
The Evening	13
The Good Soldier	17
Grunts with Grunts 24/7	17
The Erasing	20
Happy Easter	24
Doing What I Was Trained to Do	27
A Split Second	32
Pack Mentality	36
All This and a Baby Girl Too	43
Be Done with Him	47
Inept and Stubborn	53
And Now a Typhoon?	58
Almost Heaven	64
First Reflections	71
Peace Brother	75
Hey Jude	81
A Sense of Hope	85
Heaven	85
Brenda	90
New Lease on Life	100
No, Not That LBJ	105

The Way Home — 109
- The Shortest Short Timer — 109
- There's Just One Thing — 114
- Kissing the Tarmac — 119
- Home — 123

The PTSD Years — 127
- "But You Seem So Normal" — 127
- The 1970s — 128
- The 1980s — 128
- The 1990s — 129
- Here We Go Again — 130
- The Wall, April 27, 2004 — 134
- Steve — 137

Going Back, 2009 — 139
- Equatorial Hotel — 139
- War Remnants Museum — 140
- Roses on the Song Bo — 144
- Celebrating Tet — 150

Making Peace with It All — 153
- Panel W 49, May 30, 2013 — 153

What Worked For Me Might Work for You — 157
- Ten Steps to Consider — 157

Acknowledgements — 163

THE LITTLE RED NOTEBOOK

I kept a diary during my tour of duty in 1968-69 with Charlie Company, 2/501st Infantry, 101st Airborne. I served in a region surrounding the city of Hue. At the end of each day, I made cryptic notes about my experiences in a three by four inch notebook. It had a red vinyl cover. The ritual of writing gave me an opportunity to vent my frustrations and record events of the day, both good and bad.

The Little Red Notebook lived in the upper left shirt pocket of my jungle fatigues, right over my heart. I did everything I could to protect it from the ravages of combat. Somehow it survived river crossings, monsoon rains, and even a typhoon. When I returned home, I put it in the bottom drawer of my vintage oak roll top desk, where it remained unread for forty years.

The Little Red Notebook deserved more than that.

The Letters

All 224 letters I wrote during the war and sent home to my family and my fiancée, Karen Koreski, were saved. They were eventually given to me about twenty years ago. I put them straight into storage in my garage. I had no interest in reading them because the very idea made me too uncomfortable.

Things changed in 2006 when I began seeing a counselor for Post Traumatic Stress Disorder (PTSD). He asked me to read the letters along with The Little Red Notebook as a starting point in my therapy. After arranging them in sequence, I began reading with no sense of what to expect.

It was surreal. At times I didn't know this young infantryman at all. He thought Nixon was a good President? He could justify torturing and even killing civilians? *My god, that couldn't have been me.* But there it was… page after page…like it or not.

The contents of my letters contrasted with The Little Red Notebook's account of events. For instance, letters home included information on a range of topics, giving a general sense of what happened. Graphic details of combat, on the other hand, were confined to my Notebook. Sometimes they were referenced by only one or two key words… as if writing the facts was just too hard to admit to myself. When I did divulge specifics in letters, I was often responding to a question from home or I just needed to vent.

There were also significant events that I came across, ones that I had put out of my mind for decades—even the deaths of some of my closest buddies. Reading about them gave me a jolt. A sense of disbelief came over me. Sometimes I had to read the same sentence several times. As painful as the process was, I knew I had to keep reading, as it was an essential exercise in the healing process. Portions describing combat were often too painful. So I paced myself, taking more than a year to read the contents of every letter and all of the passages in the Notebook.

An unexpected benefit from the exercise was it enhanced my ability to recall things. The more I read, the more it triggered memories of lesser, but important details… filling in gaps of information long forgotten.

Through it all, I discovered four "ingredients" that had fostered my PTSD:

Sorrow I witnessed forty-nine of my buddies dying at the hands of the enemy.
Regret I killed eight or more enemy soldiers in combat.
Shame I jointly participated in the torture of enemy soldiers and civilians.
Guilt Why did I survive, when so many other deserving buddies did not?

Identifying these ingredients completed the first step towards my recovery. Resolving each one in my mind was another matter. In fact, it has taken several years, and the process may never completely end. But I am seeing results, and peace of mind is on the horizon.

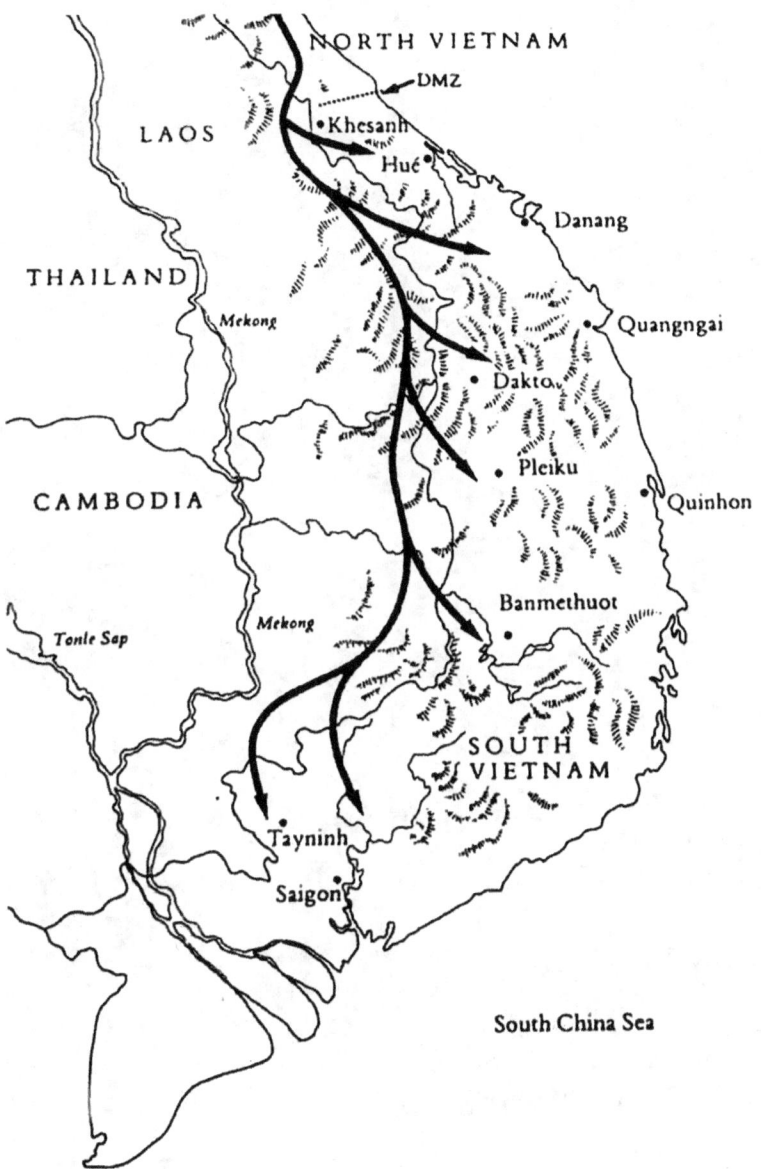

Ho Chi Minh Trail, South Vietnam, 1968

Thua Thien Province military operations, 1968

SO THIS IS COMBAT

March 24, 1968

I went by chopper to Charlie Company at 10:30 in the morning and all shit broke loose at 11:00. We were moving up a ridge and several snipers opened up killing 4 guys and wounding several others. I have never been so scared in my life because I had to walk point in the afternoon. Fuck this war.

The Morning

Packed to the gills with ammo, C-rations and five canteens of water, we struggled under the weight of our sixty-pound rucksacks to board the Huey helicopter, enveloped in rusty red haze. Sweat ran down our faces like miniature streams, creating jagged streaks on our dust-powdered cheeks. We sat in nervous silence with our legs dangling out over the edge of the chopper—two of us on each side, adjacent to the door gunners crouched behind their fifty-caliber machine guns. We turned and looked at one another as the rotor blades picked up speed and began to bite into the heavy air. My heart was pounding in sync with the distinctive "whop, whop, whop" resonating in my ears as I thought about how I would react in combat. Would I be a coward and run? Or would I be a man and take the enemy head on?

I had no fucking idea.

The ninety-mile per hour downdraft churned up a small dust storm on the chopper pad, making it even more difficult to breathe. As we lifted off and made a gradual turn towards the northeast, Camp Sally slowly disappeared into the morning mist. With an increase in altitude, we gazed down at the rice paddies below, pocked with craters from hundreds of bombs and artillery shells. The largest craters, created by thousand-pound bombs dropped from B-52s, looked like perfectly round lakes randomly dotting the countryside. They were filled with iridescent colored water caused by chemicals in the explosives. The pockmarked landform ended abruptly as the chopper crossed the foothills, gained more altitude, and headed due west about eight "clicks" (kilometers) from the ancient city of Hue. The Thien Thu Mountains below were covered with a dense green jungle canopy, interrupted from time to time by brown blotches resulting from Agent Orange defoliant drops.

The wind blowing in my face and whistling through my helmet was refreshingly cool, lulling me into a brief moment of reflection. The day had started before 6:00 am with a jolt when First Sergeant Brown, the former heavyweight boxing champion of Fort Campbell, Kentucky, woke up the new replacements, (or "cherries," as we were called) by banging on a garbage can with a baseball bat, screaming, "Get your lazy asses up and out to the chopper pad. We have a shitload of casualties coming in." We threw on our jungle fatigues and ran out to meet the incoming medivak helicopters on a morning that was already hot and steamy.

While our group put the wounded on stretchers and took them to the hospital tent, four of us were told to carry the two dark green body bags to another nearby tent. There, in the first hour of the day of March 24, 1968, Privates Barker, Hayden, Martin, and I carefully unzipped the bags, lifted the lifeless forms out, and laid each one on a table. I worked with Barker, a former Detroit street gang member. His deep brown eyes were set against his ebony skin. He was speechless, in contrast to the evening before, when he claimed he killed somebody back home in a street fight. Everyone had believed him because he delivered his story with so much conviction.

We gently removed all of the equipment and clothing from each soldier and stacked everything in a pile oozing with body fluids and blood. Without clothes, their reasons for dying became obvious. Bullet holes the size of quarters, probably from Russian-made AK-47s, riddled both bodies. A huge gash had opened the belly of the guy in front of me. Try as I might, it was impossible to ignore the hot dog sized link of intestine protruding out like a headless, cream-colored snake. An earthy stench filled the stifling air inside the tent and we all began to gag with each breath. Their pale naked forms covered in blood and grit resembled zombies from some B horror film. I knew that from that moment on, I would never be able to erase these images from my mind.

The zipper got stuck closing the body bag just as I was pulling it over the chin of the slain soldier. As I hesitated, I noticed Barker was frozen in place, staring at the floor of the tent. It seemed strange for someone who claimed to have killed a man to be so overwhelmed.

Hayden, a lanky and affable Nebraskan with a lily white complexion and rose colored cheeks, stopped working on his soldier and offered to help with the zipper. Shaking my head, I declined his assistance and pulled the zipper down the body, releasing an even stronger odor.

"Jesus fucking Christ…" I said in a low voice.

When the zipper finally broke free, I closed the bag and tried to help Hayden and Martin complete their work on the other victim. Martin, no more than five foot five, spoke with a thick Southern accent, waved me off, saying, "Man, we've got it under fucking control."

With that, I spun around and headed out of the tent to get some fresh air. Hayden was on my heels. Gulping in one breath after another, I began to feel faint and sank to the ground, all the while thinking about the grief awaiting the family and friends of these soldiers back home. Hayden plopped himself down beside and sighed, "So this is how it ends, man—you're nineteen years old and haven't even started living your life, some gook pumps five rounds into you, and it's fucking over. This is just so messed up, man, and the really shitty thing is we could be next."

"You can't think that. We gotta stay positive," I countered.

My newly assigned unit, Charlie Company, 2/501st Infantry, 101st Airborne Division, had endured nearly nonstop combat for the past week. It was rumored six had been killed yesterday alone. Essential equipment such as backpacks, weapons, gas masks, ammo belts, and poncho liners were in short supply. Consequently, the cherries were faced with a morbid form of recycling. Armed with soap and brushes, we scrubbed every usable item in futile attempt to get rid of the stench made worse by the tropical heat. The equipment was left to dry in the morning sun.

We washed up as best we could, but found the sweet aroma of Ivory Soap just wasn't strong enough to remove the lingering scent of death. Eating breakfast so soon after finishing the cleaning detail wasn't the best timing, but we had to get some food into our bellies before heading out to join second platoon. Sure enough, the sight and smell of oatmeal, eggs and bacon as we stood in the chow line triggered instant nausea. So all four of us settled for some coffee and bread well away from the mess tent.

As the chopper slowly descended in the lush mountains, I could see a small Landing Zone (LZ) had been cleared in the jungle. When we were within five hundred meters, the LZ appeared to be nothing more than the edge of a bomb crater. Hayden and I scooted forward so that our feet were on the skids. This position would allow us to exit the chopper as quickly as possible as it hovered two meters above the tortured landscape. The door gunners opened up their fifty caliber machine guns with short bursts into the distant hillsides to provide cover for our landing. Hayden and I looked over our shoulders, smiled with our thumbs pointed up, and yelled "Good luck!" in unison to Barker and Martin. They responded with forced grins and gave us the thumbs up sign in return.

Try as we might, there was no way to hide that we were four scared motherfuckers.

Seconds later, I leapt through the air much like when I was a long jumper on the Woodland High School track team. However, the weight of my backpack, water, and weapons cut short my planned trajectory, slamming me into the ground, knocking my helmet off and forcing the air out of my lungs like collapsing billows. I gasped for air and inhaled dust and debris kicked up by the Huey as it strained to gain altitude.

When the visibility began to improve, I got up on my knees and surveyed the landscape. Hayden was squatting not more than five meters to my left. As our eyes met, I heard for the first time the distinctive "pop" sound made by a rifle when fired directly at you. Shots were coming from a nearby ridge to my east. He suddenly slumped forward and collapsed.

"Are you hit?" I yelled in disbelief. When I heard no response, I belly crawled over to him, turned his shoulders toward me and asked, "Are you OK, man?" He only groaned and coughed up a thick layer of blood that ran down his chin like a Hawaiian lava flow. I dragged him a few meters over to a boulder screaming "Medic! Medic!" But the continuous explosions from incoming mortar rounds snuffed out my plea for help.

I tore away his blood-saturated shirt and stuffed it into the two-inch hole on the left side of his chest in an attempt to stop the bleeding. In a matter of seconds, all of the color left his face and he went limp in my arms. I grasped his shoulders in my hands. "Hang on! Hang on!" I shouted. But when I checked the pulse in his neck, I found nothing. After pausing to say a prayer for a guy I never really knew, I gently laid PFC Hayden down next to the rock and tried to figure out my next move.

Hue and the Perfume River from a Huey door

The Afternoon

From what I could gather, Charlie Company was pinned down by a combination of small arms fire, RPGs (rocket propelled grenades) and mortars launched from the dense hills above us. But were we trying to move forward or trying to just hold our position? Where in the hell was second platoon?

Everything was out of control.

Explosions followed by the screams of soldiers being hit by shrapnel went on and on. The air was so thick with sulfurous smoke it penetrated my taste buds. I hunkered down between two rocks and tried to burrow as deeply as possible into the earth to protect myself. I was completely consumed by fear as a piece of shrapnel glanced off the rock, zinged past my right ear and buried itself in the dirt next to my cheek. Adrenaline surged through my body and my limbs began to shake violently. I grabbed my lower legs and I pulled my knees to my chest to try and stop the convulsions. I closed my eyes and forced myself to think about Karen and waited for the attack to end. Images of our relationship raced through my head like a video on fast forward. Eventually, the attack ended and my muscles began to relax.

I crawled up the hillside to a rock formation that offered more shelter and began gulping water from one of my canteens. I slipped off my backpack, peered inside, found a can of peaches in my C-rations, and immediately downed them. The sweet nectar soothed my throat, which was parched by dust and smoke. I closed my eyes to gather my thoughts and tried to focus on just keeping my wits.

I finally heard voices in the distance. Was that second platoon? I crawled forward to a ledge that would offer a better vantage point and began to smell a strange earthy odor. I scanned the foreground from my left to right and then looked straight down. I recoiled and vomited in one continuous motion. Just two meters below me was a soldier with the top of his head torn apart, brains fully exposed like a bowl of fresh pasta, with the overflow dripping down his neck over a silver chain. Was it a St. Christopher medal? Could it be Martin? Jesus fucking Christ! I slid back down the ledge, hugged the rock for comfort, and refused to believe it was him. But all the while, I knew the truth in my heart.

A few minutes later, from seemingly out of nowhere, the young men of second platoon emerged from the underbrush and rocks. Their drawn faces reflected a mixture of fatigue and shock. Some were hunched over with fresh shrapnel wounds, while others were reloading their weapons. Everyone was in a state of transition between the last attack and the next one.

The sound of Huey blades drew my attention to the sky. The medivak landed and several guys quickly collected the wounded for their flight to the hospital in Phu Bai, a few clicks east of Hue. While the wounded were in pain, many of them were also smiling, knowing they were soon to leave our own little bit of hell. The chopper was in and out in less than a minute, and another descended moments later to pick up two moss green body bags lying side-by-side next to a mortar crater. I knelt down, spread my arms, placed a hand on each bag, and said a final prayer for Hayden and Martin. To think, less than two hours ago we were in Camp Sally joking around about our chances of survival.

Sgt. Sierra, my squad leader, was a skinny redhead from Texas with dark brown beady eyes that constantly shifted back and forth as he introduced himself. He assumed a certain posture when he was giving orders: helmet tilted back and hands on his hips. The combination indicated a bit of cockiness, and I sensed that being a sergeant in the 101st Airborne Division was the high point in his young life.

Sierra gestured to the soldiers behind him and said, "Before the gooks try to blow us away again, you gotta meet the squad. Guys, this is Hansen, our brand new cherry. He's from Washington State, just like Ogee and Sgt. Beaty. Sgt. Otto, from Pennsylvania, is over there by the rock. Hansen, the big fucker there with the M-60 is Cudnik from New York. That there is Coble, our boy from Arkansas. And you got Dunlap from Ohio sitting on his ass, as always. Last and least, over there is fuck-face Youngblood from fucking south Texas."

Each one of them quietly nodded their heads, mumbled a welcoming remark, and looked too battle weary to do anything more.

Without looking at me, Sierra barked out, "Hansen, since you are the newest cherry you will be on point. Got it?"

I just nodded in disbelief, feeling completely expendable. Me, on point! Was he serious? Jesus Christ, I just got here and I don't know what the hell I am doing! I couldn't believe my ears.

Having point meant that you took the most forward position and blazed the trail. Everyone dreaded point because you were the most vulnerable to getting shot, setting off a trip wire to a bomb, stepping on a mine, or falling into a pit full of punji sticks (razor sharp bamboo shoots coated in fecal matter). Then, it dawned on me. It was my rite of passage into the third squad, second platoon, Charlie Company—simple as that.

Lt. Santos, our platoon leader, gathered all three squads of six men each around him. He was a New Yorker from Queens and a product of West Point. He had managed to keep his uniform relatively clean while everyone else looked like shit warmed over. In a calm and deliberate manner, he laid out a strategy to lead us up the ravine and to the relative safety of the ridge top. "Guys, we have to make it to the ridge before nightfall. First platoon will be on the right flank, second platoon on the left, and third will bring up the rear. Saddle up and take your positions as fast as you fucking can."

But before I had led my squad two hundred meters up the hill, I heard the distant "thunk" sound of a mortar being fired from the ridgeline directly to our south, then another, and another. As I scrambled for cover, I could hear "incoming" shouted up and down the ravine. We were sitting ducks again, with only a few rocks for protection. Within a second, the mortar rounds were hissing down, with each explosion punctuated by screams and shouts. Shrapnel and debris flew in every direction, tearing through arms, legs and torsos in a random manner.

I hugged the lowest piece of ground I could find and buried my face deep in the dirt, twisting it sideways just enough to breathe.

All I could do was pray it wasn't my turn and listen to the creepy rhythm of the mortar attack: thunk… silence… hiss… explosion… screams. Then, in a few seconds, the hellish sequence would start up again. The unrelenting pattern of sound drove me fucking nuts.

Within a few minutes, the attack ended as quickly as it started. The only sounds now were the moans coming from Charlie Company's freshly wounded troops awaiting transport back to Phu Bai.

Sgt. Sierra picked himself up, brushed the dirt from his fatigues and said, "Hansen, if you thought today has been tough, you ain't seen nothing yet. We took way more KIA's (killed in action) during Tet in Hue. It was so fucking bad that I lost count of the dead."

On those encouraging words, I gave him a nod, took my position on point again, and started creeping up the steep hillside. I wondered just how long I would last in this blistering heat. Small bushes, scrubby trees, and boulders dotted the landscape, providing perfect cover for the enemy. My mind was on full alert, tapping into all of my senses. I tried to feel the ground carefully with my toes despite the clunky steel-toed-jungle boots. My eyes darted from side to side, and I tried to listen for the slightest sound that would indicate movement ahead of me. The only thing I could hear *right now* was my heart pounding in my chest—more from fear, perhaps, than the effort to climb up the steep slope.

About half way up the hill, Lt. Santos ordered us to stop and wait for an air strike that Captain Johnson, our commanding officer, had just called in. The strategy, he explained, was to take out any remaining enemy positions on the terrain above us so we could make safe passage to the top of the ridge. I loved the idea, but why didn't they do this earlier? Maybe, it could have prevented some of the carnage? I just didn't get it.

Soon, the roar of two Navy F-4 Phantom jets from an aircraft carrier, stationed nearby in the South China Sea, could be heard in the distance. Loaded with five hundred-pound bombs and lethal twenty-millimeter cannons, the jets circled overhead. It was essential the pilots knew precisely where Charlie Company was in relation to the suspected enemy positions. In the mixture of mangled trees, shrubs, and rocky terrain, it was nearly impossible, flying at four hundred miles per hour, to spot us, so we used lavender-colored smoke grenades to outline our location. Several of the guys in the most forward positions tossed the grenades as far as they could in front of our unit. The colorful smoke spewed into the sky and we waited for the air strike to commence.

It didn't matter if it was bad communication between the CO's radio operator and the offshore Navy command, or if there was a change in wind direction; the results were tragic all the same. As the two Phantoms swooped down spraying their explosive rounds ten meters apart in a checkerboard pattern, *Charlie Company* became the unintended target. Instead of hitting enemy positions with cannon fire, they nailed us—all three fucking platoons in less than five seconds. I was sickened to turn and see what appeared to be Barker, just a few meters behind me, lying motionless on some rocks with his helmet torn to bits. Would I be next?

When the Phantoms finished their first pass and turned to make their bombing run, I could hear the CO in the distance shouting on the radio, "Terminate the mission… you are on the wrong side of the smoke!" But it was too late: three more were killed and ten wounded.

The military called this a "friendly fire" incident. To me, it was the mother of all fuck-ups.

It took three more medivak operations before what was left of Charlie Company could continue working our way up the hill. Despite our exhaustion, we moved at a fast pace, just to get the hell out of the ravine into a safer position.

Medivak chopper attempting a rescue above a triple canopy jungle

The Evening

About 7:00 pm, I was the first to reach the top of the ridge, and I was stunned with the view. There it was, the South China Sea, not more than fifteen kilometers to the east, shimmering in the mango colored light of the setting sun. Tears welled up in my eyes. How could a scene this breathtaking be viewed from a place so tortured by war?

Once we were on the ridgeline, Charlie Company took up perimeter positions and began digging foxholes in the hard rocky soil. Ogee, our company medic from Wenatchee, Washington, shuffled over and started to dig his hole next to mine. He looked like shit, with dirt caked on his face and torn, blood-spattered fatigues hanging from his frame. As he pushed his shovel into the dirt, I could tell he had little strength left after the grueling day.

"Take a break man, I'll help you as soon as I finish mine," I offered. After hesitating for a moment, Ogee dropped to his knees, covered his face with his hands and wept.

As the darkness began to settle in, it was strangely peaceful. Everyone was quiet as we ate some chow and had a quick smoke. A soothing rain began to fall. I looked into the ebony sky and let the cool drops wash the filth from my face and hands. While it was refreshing, I was quickly overcome with the emotions of the day. What in the hell had I gotten myself into? What were the chances of surviving another day like this, let alone eleven more months?

My guard duty didn't start for two hours, so I got under my poncho liner and peered over the edge of my foxhole to Ogee. I said, "So, this is combat…"

"Yeah, man, and you passed your first test. You're an official Charlie Company grunt now—tried and true—for what it's worth." After pausing for a moment, he added with a chuckle, "and that ain't a whole hell of a lot." Moments later, Ogee closed his eyes, and was out for the night.

Curling up in a fetal position, I thought about what Ogee said. Yes, I was now a grunt, a tough motherfucker who had come face-to-face with the enemy and prevailed. I had proven my manhood and was now a card-carrying member of Charlie Company. For my efforts, the

Army would award me the Combat Infantryman's Badge, an image of an American Revolutionary War long rifle against a rectangular bright blue background. Larger than all other decorations, I would wear the cloth version proudly above my left breast pocket of my jungle fatigues. It would be my badge of courage.

The sun shone brightly the next morning after an uneventful night pulling guard duty every two hours. We spent the day cleaning our weapons, resting up and awaiting our next mission.

"So Hansen, what do you think about all of this?" Sierra said as he plopped himself down next to my foxhole, offering me a cup of lukewarm Folger's Instant Coffee.

"You mean our mission?"

"Yeah, what do you think about being a grunt in the 101st Airborne now?" Sierra said, pushing the brim of his helmet well above his brow. "Is it what you expected?"

"Well, Sierra, I don't know what the fuck to think right now. My head is still spinning. I do have a question, though. Now that we have taken this hill and controlled it, what happens next?"

"We will leave this fucking hill tomorrow and the gooks will move back in."

"You mean after all of the sacrifices Charlie Company just made, we are going to fucking walk away and start over somewhere else?"

"That's it, man," Sierra declared. "That's how we fight this fucking war. Take a hill one day and give it up the next. Kind of fucked up, isn't it?"

"So what is the point of taking the hill in the first place?"

"To kill as many gooks as we can. That's our mission… pure and simple," Sierra replied with a smirk.

"But aren't there millions of gooks? I mean, where will this all end?"

"Hansen, that's why this war is about survival—no more, no less. The way I look at it, we are here to kill commies and get back home in one piece. Simple as that."

All told, sixteen members of Charlie Company were killed from March 22nd-24th. Countless others were wounded.

March 27, 1968

Dear Family,
I am learning one heck of a lot about myself here in the boonies. For one thing, I know I've seen what Hell must really be like. When I get back to "The World" and Karen I know for sure that I will always try my very hardest at everything I do. You really appreciate living when you make it one day after the next and from firefight to firefight. Each night I am so thankful that I was fortunate to make it when so many don't. Worrying about me won't do any good, so don't waste your time. I have a buddy from Wenatchee (our medic) who I stick with. We both depend on each other—he's made it six months without a scratch. We will be a good team

Your loving son,
Jim

Wounded soldier lifted out to a Huey through trees and vines

THE GOOD SOLDIER

April 3, 1968

Had a 10-click patrol and it ended up being 20 all told. It was a SOB!

Grunts with Grunts 24/7

Days dragged on, humping up and down the vast foothills and mountains of the Thau Thien Province northwest of the City of Hue. There were no roads, only small trails that seemed to begin and end for no reason. The only access to the area was by the choppers, which took us out on missions and picked us up two to three weeks later. In that time, we had little or no contact with the outside world. Mail delivery was erratic and sometimes lost along the way. The only signal within range of my small AM transistor radio was a military station in Da Nang, offering mainstream music mixed with heavily edited news from the States.

It was grunts with grunts, 24/7. A combination of fatigue, filth, depression and anger created a "survival" mindset that intensified the longer we were on a mission.

April 3, 1968

Dear Family,
Right now I'm sitting on top of our bunker on guard soaking up the sunshine and writing you. We just got back from a patrol that started at 10:00 pm last night. It's now 2:00 pm. We set up two ambushes, but no luck. Later we went through three villages and raised a little Hell. The people over here in the towns are nice as Hell to you, but as soon as you turn your back they blow up one of your buddies. Consequently, we burn their houses and shoot a lot of civilians that are suspected VC or NVA. It sounds cruel, but you just have to work it that way.

    A little kid came up to me today and tried to bum some cigarettes. I would have liked to have given him some, but his dad was probably one of the VC that killed my buddies the night before. It's just a vicious cycle and I hate it. Actually, anyone that runs from us we can shoot—women and children included, because they all know we will think they are VC if they run. However, some panic and run so they die anyway. Thank God I haven't had to do many of these village patrols, I just don't like them. It's funny how you feel about death over here—it's so easy, yet you fear your own so much. Enough of that!

    I was hoping that you can better understand what's happening over here in my letters. I'm trying to make them straight and sound, but often I would just as soon not write about it. I hope you are fine. I'm safe and well.

Love,
Jim

Crossing a canal using a Vietnamese bamboo bridge

April 11, 1968

On patrol today we killed two civilians kind of by accident. They ran and wouldn't stop so we opened up to see if they would stop. Some of the guys must have aimed a little low. Finally rained today—felt good.

The Erasing

'You VC?" Sgt. Beaty hissed to the old man, who we suspected knew more than he was letting on. We had just found an ancient French rifle buried under sacks of rice in the man's hooch. As Beaty held the frail man by his boney shoulders, there was a sense of doom in his weary eyes. His whiskey brown skin, deeply wrinkled from years in the tropical sun, drooped from his brow and cheekbones. His grey beard was so sparse you could count the individual two-inch long hairs protruding from his chin.

"No VC! No VC!" the man pleaded, shaking his head back and forth.

"You are fucking VC! You use this rifle to kill Americans! We are going to kill you with it if you don't confess," Beaty shouted.

Frightened to death, the man's entire body trembled as he kept repeating, "No VC!" Then, he slowly collapsed on the straw mat floor. The tense scene was interrupted by some shouting outside the hooch. I dashed through the open doorway to see two women bolting down the dirt path that connected the village to the nearby rice paddies.

"Dung! Dung! Dung!" (Stop, stop, stop!) I shouted.

"Hansen, shoot them, they're goddamn VC!" Sgt. Sierra barked out.

"Yeah, fucking shoot them!" Several other guys in my squad yelled.

I raised my M16 to my right shoulder, slowly placed my finger on the trigger, and then fired a warning shot over the heads of the two women. One slowed down, but the other never broke stride.

"You fucking missed them!" Sierra hissed.

I never heard my weapon fire the second time, but I felt the vibration of the round leave the casing and travel down the barrel in slow motion. Framed by the rifle sight, I saw one of the women's arms fly up in reaction, just before her body collapsed face first into the murky water of the rice paddy. The trailing woman sprinted up to her fallen friend, but was cut down in one shot from Sierra's rifle just as she jumped into the paddy.

"We got 'em both!" Sierra proclaimed.

I started walking down the path towards the women in a daze. What the hell have I done? Were they really VC? Jesus Christ! Did I just take an innocent life?

Villagers raced past me, screaming in grief. When I reached the crowd surrounding the bodies, people stepped aside as I bent down to examine my victim now covered in oozing chocolate colored mud. A sobbing woman reached down and gently lifted her head out of the muck. Using the loose fabric of her blouse, she slowly wiped the filth away, revealing the face of a child.

I was horrified.

The woman, perhaps the girl's mother, looked up with tears streaming down her face. She just gazed into my eyes. No words were needed. Her expression said it all.

"Sorry! Sorry!" I pleaded.

Another woman squatted down and examined the exit wound in the middle of the girl's chest. Staring back to me, she covered her ears and nodded toward the girl. Then, she held up both palms extending all of her fingers, closed them, raised two fingers, and waited for my response. I shook my head, not understanding what she was trying to say.

As I walked back to the village, I was dripping with sweat. My heart was pounding so loud I could hear my pulse. Now I understood:

She was twelve. She was deaf.

She was my first kill.

Sgt. Beaty grabbed my shoulders and spun me around. "Don't worry about it, man, she had it coming," he said. "The gooks all know if they run from us, they will be shot. It's no big deal."

Before nightfall, I removed the little red plastic notebook I kept in my helmet liner, and made an entry. That was the first of several steps I took to erase her from my memory. This exercise was so successful, that the incident would not resurface in my mind again for forty years, until I visited the Vietnam War Memorial in Washington, D.C.

April 12, 1968

Honey,
Probably the most interesting thing that happened today was watching some ants moving a piece of my bread about a foot or so in the last hour. I can't believe how strong they are. They just never give up.

I feel much better this morning than I did yesterday. It just wasn't a good day. I haven't felt so horrible in a long time. But today I am feeling better. I love you from the bottom of my heart and don't forget it. I prayed about 20 minutes straight last night and most of it was for you. I hope they are answered.

God Bless You,
James

Begging for candy and cigarettes along the banks of the Perfume River

April 12, 1968

Went on another patrol of 10 clicks. One of the guys hit a booby trap and it killed him instantly. We also nearly got hit by our own artillery. Such a shame to have a guy die on Easter.

Happy Easter

The morning was especially hot and brilliant. Shortly after sunrise, we went out on patrol to sweep an area close to the South China Sea and several clicks southeast of Utah Beach. The terrain was dominated by sand dunes and sparse vegetation. Reports from Command indicated little, if any, recent enemy activity in this area, so we were all feeling more relaxed than usual. My mind wandered as I slugged my way through the increasingly thick sand and thought what Easter services must be like back home.

"Happy Easter, Cudnik," I said, as our squad started climbing up a large sand dune. At six foot five, he was the biggest guy in second platoon and he seemed to carry his M-60 machine gun and ammo belts across his massive shoulders with ease. He was from the Bronx, and he was always smiling and joking around.

"Fucking A, man, isn't this just too much?" he replied. "We're hunting gooks as if it was just any other kind of day."

"Well, the war doesn't stop for anything or anybody, not even Jesus," I responded with a laugh.

"No shit, man. It won't stop for us until we get on the fucking Freedom Bird and go back to the World. I've got 167 days and a wake-up before I get the fuck out of here. How 'bout you?"

Before I could answer, I noticed out of the corner of my eye that one of the cherries, about forty meters away, was bending down and reaching for an object sticking out of the white sand.

His war stopped.

April 15, 1968

Dear Karen,
… Yesterday was Easter and, of course, we worked as usual. The company went on a search and destroy mission to a small village about 6 clicks away. Everything was going smoothly until one man in the first platoon tripped a 60-millimeter mortar booby trap. He was killed and another was badly wounded. Shortly after that, some of our own artillery rounds nearly hit us three times! All I could think of was what I did last Easter with you…

Love you and tons of affection,
James

Squad approaches suspicious civilians

April 21, 1968

We were hit by snipers and I got my first kill today—I caught two gooks in the open and got them with my 79. It was much like shooting deer (the same feeling) probably because I've developed so much hate for gooks killing my buddies. Hill and Mac both got hit 4 and 6 times respectively, but made it. Had air strikes, gunships and artillery all day and night.

Doing What I Was Trained to Do

Just as I topped a small hill, I saw two NVA soldiers across the river running diagonally to me, no more than thirty meters away. I dropped to the ground and took aim with my M-79 grenade launcher, a weapon that looks like a sawed-off shotgun. Although it was not specifically designed for a small moving target, I didn't have time to grab my M16. Instead, I aimed the 79 just ahead of the lead soldier and fired. The airborne grenade struck him in the ribcage and he collapsed. Fragments from the round must have also hit the second soldier because he dropped to his knees. The pause allowed me time to reload. He looked in my direction just before the second grenade hit him in the waist.

That moment was for every guy in Charlie Company who had gone home in a body bag. I was now a grunt to my very core—highly capable of hunting and killing the enemy, no matter how difficult the circumstances.

Adrenaline surged through my body as I jumped to my feet. I was feeling much like I did when I shot my first deer as a teenager. That was a rite of passage, for a young man where I grew up in the shadow of Mt. St. Helens, Washington. My father couldn't have been prouder of me. Now, just seven years later, I had actually shot *two* enemy soldiers. What would he say when he got the news?

Clad in their light green, tattered fatigues, they were both lying side by side, face down. Clearly, the first guy was dead from the explosion, given the crater in his upper torso that leaked blood on the dirt path. I wasn't so sure about the second soldier, so I placed my right forefinger against his neck to check for a pulse. There was nothing. The warmth of his skin made me recoil.

A small leather wallet was lying between the two bodies. I peered inside to find three-200 Dong bills. As I pulled the cash out, I noticed a small photograph wrapped in plastic. I carefully tugged away the folded sides one at a time. A black and white image of a family slowly emerged. Two small children, a boy and a girl, perhaps two and four-years old respectively, were standing in front of a young couple. The parent's arms were around each other and their children. Everyone was smiling.

My hands began to tremble so badly that I couldn't hold the picture. It dropped on the ground face up. Scooping up a handful of mud laced with fresh blood, I covered the portrait in one motion. Using the sole of my combat boot, I methodically patted down the earth, in an attempt to forever bury the haunting image.

The reality, that I had just done something that contradicted all of the psychological and social barriers against violence that I had learned growing up, began to sink in. All of the mind-altering training by the Army that told me it was "kill or be killed," and that it was "your patriotic duty to kill," had been called into question. My initial elation from getting my first enemy "kill" was replaced with numbness.

"It's OK, Hansen, they had it coming. Think about how many of our guys they killed," Ogee offered as he knelt down beside me.

"Hey man, you just killed two gooks; you gotta be proud!" Ogee persisted.

"I don't fucking know what to think right now," I said. I slowly got to my feet and wandered over and slumped against a palm tree.

My mind reeled as I looked across the rice paddy at the two men lying dead next to the river. The responsibility for killing them was on my shoulders, and I would carry it for the rest of my life. Shit, I was now a professional killer.

Charlie Company, supported by Cobra gunships and Navy F-4 Phantom jets, continued our assault through the afternoon, routing out NVA from the maze of tunnels and bunkers with hand grenades and C-4 explosives. No prisoners were taken.

When the nameless village was secure, Ogee and I sat on the remains of a wooden cart and gazed across the tortured landscape. Virtually all evidence of the community had been eliminated. Gray smoke drifted skyward where there were once neatly thatched hooches. Several religious shrines were now piles of rubble. Palm trees that provided shade from the intense tropical sun were gone. The air, once filled with the distinctive aroma of cooking food, had been replaced with the earthy smell of the dead.

"Hey, what was the body count today, man?" Ogee asked, not taking his eyes off the aftermath.

"I heard it was fifty two," I said.

"Well, we all know that's a crock of shit. Since Command typically multiplies by a factor of three, it was around… let's say fifteen or so?" Ogee speculated.

"Yeah, probably. But all that's certain is we have made Command very happy," I said.

April 23, 1968

Dear Family,
For the past three days we have really been in the action... I finally got my first confirmed kill with the M-79 day before yesterday. I saw two gooks as plain as day across the river in a clearing and nailed them. Along with about 10 air strikes (jets and helicopter gunships) we killed at least 15 gooks. However, we had only had 4 wounded...

I was so surprised that my mail is taking so long to get to you (11 days!)... I have been fine—wet, hot, insect bitten, but actually feeling fine.

Thanks for the sweet letter, Jean!

I love you all,
Jim

Sgt. Sierra gathers our squad

April 28, 1968

Finally moved into the village and found a few bodies and beaucoup bunkers and tunnels. While we were taking a break, Peterson was shot and killed by a sniper as we were sitting side by side. He was a good friend and the smartest guy in the company. We had to carry his body 400 meters to the chopper. You couldn't have found a nicer guy—never bitched about a thing.

A Split Second

I cradled his limp body in my lap as the rest of second platoon scrambled to find the sniper. The fresh dairy smell of his cream colored brains enveloped my senses as they drained out of his skull and on to my lap like huge chunks of pasta. I was ready to puke. Ogee sprinted over and examined his wound.

"Ogee, he didn't fucking deserve this!" I wailed. "Peterson was a good man and a good soldier. He should have made it through this goddamn war. This just isn't fucking right."

"I know, I know, I know..." he responded in a soothing tone.

Peterson was a psychology major at Utah State. We shared a common bond because we both were drafted after dropping a class while attending college. He wasn't like most of my other buddies. Rather than bullshitting about girls, cars, and music all the time, he loved to ponder substantive things. He would expound about world politics in one conversation and the meaning of life in the next. We didn't always agree on everything, but we loved taking positions on issues for the sake of lively banter. It helped take our minds off the war for a moment or two. Now, he was gone and the conversations would end.

Moments earlier, we were sitting on a small dike above a rice paddy sharing some C-rations. He was talking and I was eating. Bending over, I stirred my chow in my aluminum canteen holder on the ground. In less than a second, a sniper's bullet passed over my shoulders and struck him in the right side of the head.

It could have just as easily been me. It should have been me.

Dealing with the guilt and heartbreak was more than I could handle.

It went straight to my core and left me reeling—looking for something, anything, to give me comfort and hope. This time, it was nowhere to be found.

April 29, 1968

Dear Karen,
This is the first time I have had a chance to write in a few days. We are still near Hue and in the action. Yesterday was something else. We killed 4 gooks and thought we were doing fine. However, just before noon we were hit. One of the guys was blown completely apart…

…We haven't been dry for 6 days now with so many rivers to cross. All day and night we are wet.

Joan sent me the most fantastic cake yesterday! We all ate it in no time and loved it!

As the day ended, we had 4 more killed and 6 wounded. One of the guys killed was a close friend—the kind you say "hi" to and don't really know why you like each other so much. What a damn shame.

I love you Karen,
Jim

Medivak approaches south of Hue to pick up Peterson's body bag

May 5, 1968

Had a little contact last night and killed two gooks. Purdue fell asleep on guard and a gook shot him in the head. He was still alive when the medivak came in. No water or food all day and ended up drinking out of a mud puddle. It was positively miserable.

Pack Mentality

As Charlie Company continued to reel from nearly non-stop combat, I sensed there was an enemy growing *inside us*. I felt it in myself. I could see resentment and bitterness in the eyes and actions of everyone. We were sharing the same sickness.

It loomed like a dark, inky fog clinging to the ground. It would dissipate when we came into Sally for a break, and then return when we went out on the next mission. It followed us across the rice paddies, through the jungle, and into every village we swept.

Our rancor didn't manifest itself overnight. It developed, almost methodically, over several months.

It started with pessimism that grew out of the Tet Offensive, when the enemy unexpectedly kicked our ass. We suffered huge losses during the month-long event. Everyone was feeling pain. At the time, it was akin to being in the ring with Sonny Liston. A fierce body blow knocks the wind out of you with such force it's impossible to breathe, and when you look up another fist is headed straight at your face.

Three months later, we were still reeling.

We had completed nearly fifty senseless missions by now, with few measurable results. Command would order us to secure a "strategic" mountaintop. We would take several casualties in the process, only to be told to abandon the position a day or two later. We would kill an NVA soldier on an ambush one night, only to lose two buddies the next day. It was a cycle of aggravation and futility.

We were also becoming more aware of political unrest back home. Stories of student demonstrations and the debates in Congress were making their way to us via newspaper articles sent by our families and friends. We shared our perceptions about the declining level of support with mixed emotions.

Some of us, including myself, supported the protests, thinking they would eventually force Congress to pull the plug on the war. Others did not. Many deeply resented the "privileged college idealists" who thought they understood Vietnam—protesting by day and going to campus parties by night. Then there were the Young Republicans who supported the war. If they felt so passionate about it, why weren't they over here standing shoulder-to-shoulder with us, fighting the Communists?

But no matter what side of the debate we were on, few of us believed this still "undeclared war" was winnable. In fact, *winning* was an increasingly irrelevant term. *Surviving* the war seemed to be the operative word. Just focus on getting through your 365-day tour of duty unscathed.

Most of us viewed the South Vietnamese government armed forces (ARVNs) as corrupt and worthless, respectively. The Army insisted on sending out ARVNs to support us in the field. But when we came under fire, these "wannabe warriors" would scatter like fragments of metal from an exploding grenade. We were confounded by their cowardly behavior—running away from the enemy rather than defending their country. Sometimes we were ready to shoot them ourselves, to save the VC and NVA the trouble.

And what about the civilians? Wasn't the U.S. in South Vietnam to save them from the Communist north? Yet did any of them really want us in their country? By the way they regarded and treated us, you would have thought we were carrying the plague. If that wasn't enough, you couldn't trust any of them. Time after time, we discovered villagers harboring VC. Turn your back on one of the men, women, or even the children, and it might be your last breath.

Finally, did the act of killing the enemy trigger repressed feelings we carried deep inside our souls? I didn't think so for myself, but I wasn't so sure about some of my buddies, who I witnessed mutilating the dead. Whatever it was, individually or collectively, our dark side had risen to the surface. We wore it on our faces like a medieval executioner's mask.

We were not to be messed with—not by anyone, for any reason.

On the outside we looked more like animals every day, unshaven and filthy. We couldn't bathe more than once every week or two, depending on whether it was safe when we crossed streams. The cuts on our arms and legs from sharp branches and thorns were always infected. In my case, the sores had turned into jungle rot, an aggressive and painful skin condition with scabs and oozing pus. Our fatigues were ripped to shreds and stained with sweat and blood. We looked like shit, and we didn't care. Our outward appearance was the perfect complement to how we were feeling on the inside. Hand in glove.

Of course, there was a consequence to this sickness Charlie Company shared—our conduct.

It was particularly bad following hit and run tactics by the enemy, when we took casualties and failed to launch an effective counterattack. They were clever and crafty, operating in their own backyard, and taking every advantage of our ignorance.

When we least expected it, snipers picked us off one by one, and then disappeared in a matter of seconds. Other times, from a hidden location, the VC/NVA detonated one of our Navy's unexploded five-hundred-pound bombs, killing and wounding our troops. By the time we regrouped and called in artillery or air support, the bastards were long gone. The pattern repeated itself in a variety of forms. It bugged the holy hell out of us.

Guerilla warfare—we just couldn't quite figure it out.

If the urge to exact some revenge occurred at the same time we were sweeping a village, civilians thought to be suspects were tortured and their homes set ablaze. Nothing was left unscathed, including religious shrines and historic structures, which became targets for our LAWs (light anti-tank weapons). My buddies would scream with delight as they fired their miniature bazookas, blowing objects a hundred meters away into a thousand pieces. While I participated in this activity, it ate away at me. We were destroying their culture, one rocket at a time.

Charlie Company had little patience with prisoners we captured. What the VC and NVA did not understand is their lives meant nothing to us. If they weren't quick to divulge the information we wanted, they were going to die. The process usually began with one of our squad leaders yelling directly into the face of the prisoner. "Are you VC? Where are you hiding VC? You kill American GIs?" Most could not speak any English, so the conversation was usually one way. If they didn't admit to being VC or remained silent, we kicked or struck their midsections with rifle butts. If body blows didn't yield the desired response, faces would be targeted next. If there were multiple prisoners, then the apparent leader would be singled out and "roughed up," as we put it.

A knife to the throat with enough pressure to draw blood punctuated our verbal threats. An even more effective method, however, was pressing the blade up against their exposed genitals. It was a surefire way to get a stubborn one to talk. The irony was that the prisoners often divulged little, if any, useful information. But the gruesome process made us feel better, if nothing else. Our officers rarely stepped in to stop the torture. On some level they must have realized it was a way for us to vent our frustrations, and permitting the torture might prevent a total meltdown, in which an entire village might be slaughtered.

Sometimes badly wounded prisoners were killed. This was justified because we needed to conserve medical supplies and it was risky having prisoners around. If they were able to escape, they might try to take one of us out. In reality, we didn't want to be bothered to take care of some S.O.B. who had just tried to kill us. They didn't deserve to live, we did. That was the Charlie Company mantra.

I wanted nothing to do with harassing villagers and burning their homes or torturing and killing prisoners. I didn't have the stomach for it. Yet, there I was, going along with the pack, taking an occasional swipe with the butt of my M16. Behaving in this manner would have been unthinkable before combat. But I had strayed a long way from the idealistic young college student I was before being drafted months earlier.

The Army provided me with the means and the authority to kill the enemy. By their definition, I was a good soldier because I did what I was told. Along the way, I witnessed enough violence against my buddies to make me want to retaliate. While I tried to avoid that temptation at a personal level, I tolerated others doing it.

My transition from civilian to soldier was regressive. Whatever I had become as an infantryman did not measure up to the level of character I had as a civilian. I was now less of a man. My sense of self-respect suffered.

My fiancée, Karen, and our families would be horrified if they knew the real truth. But I would never let that happen. I would bury all of those memories forever.

The peace of mind I would seek later was more than forty years away.

May 10, 1968

Dear Karen
...Your letter about my experiences over here really shook me up. There is such a difference in war, and revenge I guess is the partial answer. What else can it be? I don't really know.

I don't feel bad about killing because of my dead friends. I know it must be very hard for you to understand, but I'm just trying to do my job. When you see a gook you have to kill him with no hesitation. The more kills you get, the prouder you can be. What else can you attain over here besides staying alive? And that's the only way it can be.

My attitudes and beliefs about life haven't changed a bit, Honey. I'm the same old Jim that needs Karen more than ever! I only told you about what I had been doing because you wanted me to tell you everything.

I love you,
Jim

Ogee, Otto, Sierra and Eaves (L to R) in the upper Song Bo River

June 19, 1968

I couldn't believe that we had to walk another 20 clicks again today. Tried to talk to a woman into keeping her American baby—what a shame that this has to happen. Got back too late for chow.

All This and a Baby Girl Too

"GI, GI, you want baby? You take home?" I heard shouted from inside a hooch as we swept yet another nameless village in the Thau Thien Province. Ducking under the thatched roof and looking through the doorway, I saw a young woman all alone, naked from the waist down, squatting above a grass mat. Looking more closely, I noticed the head of a baby emerging between her legs. Following each one of her elongated grunts, she would gasp for air and then say, "GI, GI, you take baby?"

I stood in stunned silence not quite believing what I was seeing as the child slowly slid out of her. It struck me that she was using gravity to assist her, as opposed to the Western position where women lay down and must have someone help pull the baby out.

Before the head touched the mat, she cupped it in her blood-covered hands, allowing the tiny body to gently come to a rest between her bare feet. Using her teeth, she severed the umbilical cord a few inches above the baby's tummy and tied it in a knot. Turning the child over her knee, she gave it a quick swat on the butt. When the little girl began to cry, she took a cloth and gently wiped away the afterbirth from her body and cradled it in her arms. The ease with which she performed the task suggested she had done it a few times before.

The woman struggled to stand and then turned towards me with tears in her eyes saying once again, "GI, GI, you take baby?" I was still speechless as I watched the remaining amniotic fluid run down her legs and form a puddle on the mat.

"GI, GI, you marry me…take baby USA? Yes, you marry me? We go USA?" she pleaded.

"Mama san, you keep the baby. I can't take the baby," I said.

"Baby no good, baby no good. It American. It go with you… or I let die."

Now I understood. Some GI had gotten her pregnant and she was cursed to have a mixed race baby. Many women kept their babies in situations like this, but some did not, especially if they had too many children and/or too little food to go around.

"Mama san, you keep pretty baby," I said in a pleading tone. "I must go now. Please keep pretty baby."

I left the hooch before she had time to respond. As I ran back to join second platoon about two hundred meters away, I kept turning around to see if there might be anyone in the village who could help her. But there was no one to be seen.

"Where the hell have you been?" Sgt. Sierra shouted. "Choppers are coming in to take us back to Pinkie."

Just as I was about to respond, Sierra barked, "The rest of the squad is setting up a perimeter next to the paddies. Now, get your ass over there ASAP."

God, he was such a pompous little prick sometimes! Being a sergeant had long since gone to his head.

Knowing it was useless to say anything about the mama san, I took up a perimeter position with my squad and stared back at the lonely hooch in the distance, wondering what would become of the baby girl. Maybe there was an orphanage nearby? What about the hospital in Phu Bai? Sadly, there was neither the time nor the means to help her out.

The distant sound of chopper blades cutting the air signaled our pending departure was just minutes away. Shaking my head from side to side, I kept thinking about the baby and hoped to God that someone in the village would come to her rescue.

If only the American father could have been in the hooch, watching his daughter enter the world, instead of me. Maybe he would have had some sense of obligation? Who was I kidding? He was probably back in the States by now, banging his wife or girlfriend.

I had to face reality. She was just another victim of this senseless war.

June 20, 1968

Dear Karen,

The most amazing thing happened yesterday. After a 20 click long, ass dragging day, we swept a village in a pretty safe area southeast of Hue. I came across a woman actually having a baby! I mean she just squatted down and had a baby girl right in front of my eyes in a hooch!! Then, she tried to give the little baby girl to me because it had an American father. I guess over here they don't like children of more than one race so sometimes they just let them die! God, I wish somehow I could have helped her, but we had to keep moving on our next mission.

We are at Pinkie now going on another stupid search and destroy mission over the same exact area we have swept twice before… it's so fucked up over here!

Love,
James

Temporary bridge over the Song Bo River

July 27, 1968

Been in country five months now and hate it more than ever. Actually, I hate Youngblood even more than that.

Be Done with Him

For a moment or two I considered killing him. It would have been so easy, given his sleeping position. His neck was turned upward. His pasty white skin reflected the moonlight. Just one quick swipe of my eight-inch razor sharp Bowie knife across his jugular and it would have been the beginning of the end for Private Youngblood. As his artery began to gush like a geyser, I would stuff my poncho liner into his mouth to muffle his screams. Using all of my body weight, I would pin him down until he finally fell limp. Then, we all would finally be done with him. No more fuck-ups from the most worthless guy in Charlie Company. With him gone, our chances of surviving this insane war would increase exponentially. This was one of three options I would consider in the predawn hours on July 27, 1968.

Some guys always seemed to fall asleep on guard despite the risks to their buddies and themselves. No matter how much they promised to stay alert, it wasn't worth taking a chance on them if given a choice. You knew they could never be trusted. But the fact was the CO never gave us a choice in the matter. Instead, night after night it was all put up to chance by drawing straws. That evening, as dusk settled in across the coastal plain of Thau Thien Province, my luck ran out. I drew Youngblood. He had a reputation for falling asleep more than any other guy in addition to a long list of other irritating traits.

Private Youngblood, the "pride" of Port Arthur, Texas, was the kind of infantryman who never had his shit together. The first thing I noticed about him when he joined my squad weeks earlier was the way he wore his uniform. His oversized fatigues hung on his boney frame like a scarecrow. The straps of his sixty-pound rucksack were always loose, creating a constant state of imbalance. If his rucksack, ammo belt, and canteens weren't sliding off of one shoulder, they were sliding off of the other.

His perpetual state of disorder was enhanced when he attempted to walk through the jungle. As the vines snared his equipment, stretched to their limit and snapped back, he was often thrown to the ground, landing in a pile like an enormous water buffalo turd.

To make matters even worse, he always seemed distracted. Instead of pointing his M16 towards the ground as was standard procedure, he carried it haphazardly with no regard for his fellow soldier. But the most frightening thing was he left the safety off, increasing the likelihood of shooting one of us in the back. You always wanted to make sure you were *following* Youngblood. It was like being with a rebellious two year-old who had his finger looped through a hand grenade pin. We were all just counting the days until we could get rid of him.

Without saying a word, Youngblood and I gathered up our equipment, including M16s, extra ammo belts, water, grenades, shovels, and a PRC-25 radio. As we slowly made our way to the Charlie Company perimeter in the dim light, I could see the other guys making faces, pointing at Youngblood, and gesturing to me, as they celebrated not having to go with him. Just as I stepped carefully over one of our trip wires attached to a flare, I turned to caution Youngblood. But it was already too late. In that brief moment, he managed to snag the wire with his rifle butt. The phosphorous-filled flare popped and suddenly a miniature Fourth of July fireworks display was ignited, silhouetting my entire squad in the darkness.

"What the fuck, Youngblood?" I hissed, careful not to raise my voice. "How could you not see the goddman wire? You are going to get the whole fucking company killed. Jesus fucking Christ!"

"I... I... I... I... I... don't know what happened," he stammered in his deep southeastern Texas drawl.

"Well, fucking pay attention!" We've got one more wire to go and it's attached to a goddamn Claymore."

I took a deep breath and thought that if the VC didn't know where we were earlier, surely they knew now. After the flare died down, we made our way across the sand dunes to a point about one hundred meters outside the perimeter.

Digging a foxhole in the configuration of a giant golf divot about three meters wide in coarse sand, Youngblood and I began to set up our LP (listening post). LPs were early warning devices. The Army thought they were an effective method to detect movement of the enemy during the night before they reached a company perimeter. While the concept was sound, it didn't take into consideration the incredible risk for the soldiers in the LP. We were literally sitting ducks out there. If the VC happened to come around, we were fucked.

Youngblood and I discussed the shift schedule and agreed I would take the first hour. Just before falling asleep he said, "You don't have to worry man, I've got some hard candy to keep me awake." Not feeling the least bit reassured, I settled into the routine of calling in time checks to our CO's radioman every thirty minutes. I didn't mind making the calls because it helped keep me alert. I also chewed M&Ms and perfected the art of smoking under my poncho liner without letting any light escape. And I spent lots of time fantasizing about what I would do if I survived the war. Everything came to mind, from marrying my fiancée, Karen, to sports cars, to the latest pictures in Playboy magazine I kept tucked inside my helmet. Masturbation was not out of the question, if nothing else worked.

Through the first two shifts, Youngblood seemed to be fairly alert, so it made it easier for me to fall asleep quickly when it came my turn. Perhaps an hour or more later, I was awakened by his snoring. I immediately grabbed the radio and called in a time check, to the relief of the Charlie Company radioman who was worried when he hadn't heard from us. It was at that point that I considered, but passed, on the first option, of slicing his aorta.

Instead, I took the barrel of my M16, chilled by the dew of the night, and placed it on Youngblood's alabaster neck. Even *that* sensation didn't cause him to stir. So, I jammed the end of the barrel deeply into the soft skin under his jaw. Unable to scream because he couldn't open his mouth, I only heard a creepy gurgle come from his throat. I kept the pressure steady as he struggled to breathe and tears began to run down his cheeks.

"You are a fucking dead man, Youngblood," I said in a strained whisper. I lessened the pressure so he could respond.

"But I wasn't asleep; I was just resting my eyes," he replied.

"Youngblood, you are a lying sack of shit," I jammed the barrel back under his jaw with even more force, tearing the tender tissue. I watched blood begin to flow from the wound and slowly trickle down the barrel. His eyes began to bulge out of his sockets, resembling Wile E. Coyote in a confrontation with the Road Runner.

For some time, I went back and forth in my mind whether I should simply pull the trigger and be done with him. However, as my stoic Danish temperament gradually returned, I realized I would have to pass on this option as well. It just wasn't worth the risk of spending a few years in a military prison. I eventually withdrew my rifle, sunk back on my side of the foxhole, and tried to gather myself.

Neither of us spoke for perhaps an hour or more as we stared out into the starry tropical sky. Finally, the silence was interrupted by the faint sound of his snoring. It was at that point I understood, that unlike the rest of the guys in Charlie Company, Youngblood truly didn't have any regard for life, even his own. How could this be? It was something I could not fathom.

Looking down at the knife on my belt for a few moments, and then over to my M16, resting against the side of the foxhole, I decided to go with my third and final option. I would let him live… at least for now.

At the first light of day, we silently gathered our equipment and made our way back across the dunes. Just before reaching the perimeter, he stopped and stared down at the ripples in the sand. Then, without looking up, he said in a barely audible voice, "I'm sorry, man." I just stared at this pathetic excuse for an infantryman and couldn't find the words to respond.

A week or so later, when we returned to Camp Sally for a much needed break, there was an MP (military policeman) standing next to the chopper pad as we landed. He arrested Private Youngblood and led him away in handcuffs. While we never officially learned why was sent back to the States, but rumor had it that he had committed some kind of felony before he came to Nam. The actual reason for his departure never mattered much to any of us. Youngblood was there no more. Our chances of surviving the war had just gone up a couple of notches. That realization put a little smile on every face in second platoon for a moment or two.

July 31, 1968

Dear Family,
I have learned so much about the nature of people over here. There is this guy named Youngblood who serves in my squad. He is completely worthless in almost every imaginable way. The other night he fell asleep when we were on an LP. I got so mad because he didn't care about my life or even his own. I just can't imagine being that way. It's crazy. I felt like killing him.

I ran into an old friend from AIT who is in the 1/501st Infantry, Sam Fugitt. We talked for hours and I found out that about 15 of my best friends had been killed. However, several, like Sam, are fine and healthy.

Well, when this letter arrives I'll have just under 7 months left. Thanks for the package today. I loved the crab!

I think we may be going to A-Shau Valley soon—so goes the latest gossip.

See you later,
Jim

Torching a civilian's hooch

August 6, 1968

Raining hard and walked in a stream to cover our tracks. Sgt. Campbell had us lost all day and my morale couldn't get much lower. Finally found the rest of the Company tonight and to beat everything they were all dry sitting under their ponchos having dinner.

Inept and Stubborn

"Sarge, the terrain ahead doesn't match our topo map. We're supposed to be approaching a river right now and there should be a couple of mountains off to the west. With all due respect, we're headed in the wrong direction," I said with growing frustration in my voice.

Campbell snapped, "Hansen, you are just fucking wrong. I know where we are. Now call in our coordinates again to Command and see if they can confirm our location."

"Okay, Sarge. Blue Falcon One. Blue Falcon One, this is Charlie Mango, over," I said.

"Blue Falcon One, go ahead…"

"We need coordinates confirmation."

"Ten-four. Wait one."

Sure enough, when Command checked the positions of first and third platoons and called me back, it was clear that coordinates didn't match up. We were fucking lost again.

"Jesus H. Christ," Sgt. Campbell hissed.

The truth be told, it wasn't all his fault. The laminated topographic maps the Army issued were based on earlier French cartography. They were so inaccurate at times that one of our favorite sayings was: "If only the French could make maps like their wine." We often came across mountains where there should have been a valley or two rivers when there should have been one. As a result, leading a platoon successfully through the mountains west of Hue was difficult, even without the enemy attacking. Good platoon leaders had to be savvy about geography and be open to the opinions of others. Campbell fell short in both respects.

As the platoon RTO (radio operator) at that time, I never left his side during a mission. Even though I had refined navigation skills from hiking and climbing the Cascade Mountains of Washington State, he rarely sought my opinion or the squad leaders who had similar skills. Instead, he tried to figure out everything on his own.

Campbell was just a stubborn S.O.B.

What second platoon desperately needed at this point was Lt. Santos back. He had left a few weeks earlier on emergency leave to take care of a family matter in New York City. Master Sgt. Campbell was brought in to be our interim platoon leader. There was no comparison to his leadership capabilities between the two. First lieutenant Santos was a West Point graduate and Campbell was a twenty-five year career soldier. While all of that experience should have been an asset, it never seemed to have translated. Every guy in the Company had the greatest respect for Santos and was counting the days until his return.

Two days later, on August 6th, it happened again. By my calculation, it was the eighth incident in three weeks. When Campbell finally acknowledged we were headed in the wrong direction, it required backtracking ten clicks through a fierce rainstorm. Not only were we exhausted and soaked upon our return to base camp, we had become the laughingstock of Charlie Company. We all were ready to kill him. It was just a matter of how and when. If his attitude somehow magically changed, perhaps we might give him a break. But that was never going to happen.

As we were digging in that night and out of earshot of Campbell, the debate began. Whether we were serious or not about our intent didn't really matter so much at this point. It just felt good to consider a quick and dramatic solution to our problem.

"Should we shoot him during a firefight, or frag him (kill him with a hand grenade) while he's sleeping?" Sgt. Beaty asked.

"Way too risky to frag him out here in the boonies. We'd have to wait until we got back to Sally and catch him alone in his bunker at night," Sgt. Sierra said.

"And if we shoot him we can't use an M16 'cause the wound would be too small for an AK. If we only had one from the gook stash we found last week, we could take care of him right away," I added.

The debate went on another day or two but in the end his life was spared when fate intervened. On the morning of August 8th, the VC launched a mortar attack about seven clicks north of Firebase Bastogne. As we scrambled up the mountainside for cover, Campbell broke his ankle when he tripped over a rock. He was medivaked out following the attack, sent to Japan to recover, and we never saw him again.

A collective cheer could he heard across the LZ as his chopper disappeared over the horizon.

August 10, 1968

Dear Family,
I'm feeling much better now that I've been in Sally two days. My jungle rot has been going away steadily. I've been eating like a hog having hot chow and cold milk, so my health is much better.

I got two packages from you yesterday and one from Judy so I'm really squared away food-wise.

Karen ended up getting an A in her Marine Biology course at the University of Hawaii. She amazes me how hard she works for her grades. I wish I had her drive.

Mom, I really slipped up this year and forgot to send you at least a "Happy Birthday letter." I did have Dad buy you something from me to you but as far as a special letter from me, I blew it. As late as it will be—HAPPY BIRTHDAY to the best Mom a guy could ever have or hope to have.

You have given me guidance for my whole life that has helped me over the roughest obstacles. In return, I have never given back near enough appreciation. Especially during the past six months you have been so good to me, better than any other guy's mom I know here. Thanks so very much and may God Bless You!

Happy Birthday! I love you!
Jim

Sgt. Beaty finds a giant centipede

September 8, 1968

We were given orders to cross the Song Bo late today with the river very high. I was watching from a hill when one of the guys was having trouble pulling his way across on a rope. Two of my buddies (Sierra and Beaty) jumped in and tried to give him a hand, but he let go and was swept down the river. Really a shame for a guy to drown over here. What was even worse was that he gave up.

And Now a Typhoon?

Cold drops of water fell on my forehead, ran down the bridge of my nose, and dropped into my olive green C-ration can filled with Folgers Instant Coffee. The pace was equivalent to the methodic tick of the grandfather clock in the den of my parents' home. I used the never ending supply of droplets to both cool and dilute the wretched excuse for coffee I was sipping to ward off the damp chill that had settled into the very core of my body.

Ogee and I huddled under our makeshift tent, comprised of two green rubber ponchos tied together with bootlaces. It leaked in several spots, including the one right above my head, but it was better than being out in the deluge. We sat on our poncho liners that had long since become saturated. At least it prevented the mud from oozing into our little island and making conditions even more miserable.

"You want some coffee, man?" I asked as I stirred in sugar to offset the foul taste.

Ogee sighed and said, "Sure, anything to warm up. I can't believe how fucking cold I am. It feels like it's in the fifties. When is the goddamn rain every going to stop?"

"Yeah, it's been pouring for two days straight," I said, dumping another helmet full out on the liquified soil. "That's the sixth helmet full… so it's probably rained nearly thirty fucking inches, assuming the helmet is about five inches deep."

During the first week of September, the weather took a sudden turn as a typhoon came ashore in Da Nang, a port city about forty clicks to the southeast. Blue Falcon Command in Camp Eagle instructed us to hunker down on high ground and wait it out for a day or two. Our position on a mountain ridge, eighteen clicks west of Hue, proved to be a slight advantage from a drainage standpoint, as wind driven rain sent torrents of water and debris flowing down the hillsides into the streams below.

The visibility was so poor with the heavy rain and fog, that we could hardly see the guys in the next position, about fifteen meters away. All we could do was wait it out, knowing at least we were safe from attack. We were convinced even the VC were staying put under these conditions.

By the following morning, September 8th, the typhoon had finally passed, and there were only a few lingering showers as the sun attempted to break through the heavy overcast skies. Our highest priority was to dry out our equipment while the terrain recovered from the deluge. Clearly, we knew, Command would not order us out for a couple of days until conditions improved.

We were so wrong. Orders came down calling for us to move north four clicks to a distant ridge that required crossing the upper reaches of the Song Bo River. Didn't they know the conditions we were dealing with? What in the fuck were they thinking?

We could hear the roar of the river well ahead of seeing it. When it did come into view, the Song Bo had been transformed into Vietnam's version of the Colorado River at full flood stage: a lethal undulating brown ribbon, knifing through the Kelly green jungle about thirty meters wide.

"This is so messed up, man. This is pure and simple bullshit," Sgt. Beaty muttered out of earshot of the CO.

"Fucking A. Do you think he even tried to question the order from Command?" I asked.

"No man, he's a pussy. He always does what they want so he can get a field promotion to major. There's nothing like a war to move an asshole like him quickly up the ranks," Beaty said as he lit a cigarette, inhaled and blew the smoke out of his nostrils.

Captain Hamilton, appearing to be even taller than his six-foot, four-inch frame, paused and scanned the entire Company of 110 men surrounding him, turned and silently pointed at the other side of the river. An image of Moses parting the Red Sea for his followers came to mind.

When we found the narrowest point on that reach of the river, two guys from first platoon volunteered to swim across the rope. Stripped down to their boxer shorts to reduce drag in the strong current, they just managed to make it to the other side. The current carried them downstream, and they had to hike back to secure the rope to a palm tree.

From my guard position on a rock high above the river, I watched one reluctant solider at a time begin crossing hand-over-hand. It took a tremendous amount of strength to withstand the force of the water. Some of the smaller guys were bounced along the surface, resembling human-sized "skippers," the flat, round rocks that I had tossed across Horseshoe Lake when I was a kid. As water slammed against their faces, I was fearful that some of them might panic in midstream, but within less than an hour most of first platoon had made it safely across.

Minutes later screams from the river caught my attention. One soldier was stationary in the middle of the Song Bo, holding on to the rope. It looked like it might be "Dorch." Without hesitating, Beaty and Sierra sprinted toward the crossing, tossing their rucksacks aside along the way. They dove in, swam for the rope to secure themselves, and yelled for him to hang on. Just before they reached Dorch, perhaps five meters away, he let go. In an instant, his lanky form was undulating with the current, passing over one white frothing rapid after another. Within a few seconds, he was out of sight. We were horrified and stood speechless at the river's edge.

The remainder of second platoon made an uneventful crossing. As I strained to hang on to the rope, fighting the incredible current, I kept thinking about Dorch.

Did he give up, or just lose his grip? I suspected he did the former. After months of combat many guys didn't expect to survive anyway. So why prolong fate?

At dawn the next day, we resumed our search. The CO called in a Cayuse, a small observation chopper, to assist. But it wasn't until the next day that the chopper pilot spotted him, snagged in some bushes on the edge of the river. Since second platoon was the closest, we arrived on the scene before the rest of Charlie Company.

Three days of tropical heat had bloated Dorch nearly to the bursting point. His skin, stretched beyond imagination, was an abhorrent mixture of colors ranging from red to purple to black, shining in the afternoon sun.

"Jesus Fucking Christ...," Sierra said, as he dropped to his knees in disbelief. Our squad remained motionless as we struggled to process the ghastly sight. As the light breeze blowing up the Song Bo shifted, the stench of Dorch gently settled over second platoon. Some of the guys began to gag.

"He didn't fucking deserve this," I said to Sierra. "What the hell was Command thinking when they ordered us to cross?"

"No shit. And what the fuck are they going to tell Dorch's family?" Sierra questioned.

"Yeah, how do you explain this pathetic situation?" I added.

But of course, we all knew the Army would never release the *actual* facts of his death. Soldiers were supposed to die while committing acts of heroism. Drowning was hardly honorable.

September 9, 1968

Dear Family,
The weather is improving following a typhoon, of all things. We were attempting to cross a very swift river and we had a man drown. We were using a nylon rope, but he just gave up and let go with two guys trying to save him. It was really a pitiful thing.

We didn't get our mail last time so I don't have much to converse about. I hope all is well and you get an Indian Summer this year.

Love,
Jim

NVA weapons and ammo

September 21, 1968

They sent me to the 22nd Surgery in Phu Bai because my leg was so badly infected. My right calf is a third again as big as my thigh! They may send me to Da Nang soon because it is pretty serious. Saw some doctors save a guy's life that was dead by massaging his heart. I couldn't believe it!

Almost Heaven

I wasn't hungry, filthy, exhausted or afraid.

For the first time in almost seven months of combat, I was *comfortable*—wrapped in a cocoon of cool, crisp, white cotton sheets in the 95th Evac Hospital in Da Nang. I was reveling in the moment, feeling as close to heaven as I ever could have imagined, and never wanting it to end.

Two weeks earlier, my jungle rot had continued to worsen. When I finally took my boots off for an entire day at Col Co Beach, a local R&R center 15 clicks east of Hue, my lower right leg inflated like a birthday balloon. By the end of the day, I couldn't get my boot back on and my buddies were calling me "Popeye."

"Man, what the hell happened to your fucking leg, Hansen?" Ogee asked as he bent down to take a closer look.

"I don't know what the hell is going on, but the swelling is out of control. It looks like it's gonna explode," I said.

"No shit man, we've gotta get that thing looked at by a doc ASAP. I'll tell Lt. Santos and I'm sure he will have you choppered over to the 22nd Surgery in Phu Bai," Ogee added with his deep-furrowed-brow look. I only saw that expression when he was *really* serious, which was a rarity.

I was off to Da Nang after less than two days in Phu Bai, on a 7:00 a.m. flight. They said I needed to see a skin infection specialist. Wedged into a Chinook helicopter between several wounded troops, I heard moans and screams every time we hit some turbulence during the 45-minute flight. Clearly, the severity of their wounds put my condition quickly in perspective. My infection may have been serious, but I wasn't going to die from jungle rot.

My bed was one of a hundred or more that were lined up in two neat rows in an inflatable rubber building. So much for protection from a rocket or mortar attack… The 95th Evac was the largest Army hospital in the region and my wing had no walls, offering a full view of every patient. Doctors and nurses were in constant motion, attending to the newly wounded as well as those in long-term recovery.

While it was wonderful to be away from combat for now, I hadn't escaped the war. As I scanned the ward that first morning, I could see GIs to my left and right being treated for every imaginable wound. There were guys with missing limbs, burns, infections, head injuries, and gunshot wounds. In fact, the soldier next to me was so messed up he seemed to have all of the above. It was unnerving to be surrounded by so many young men in so much pain.

When a GI suddenly went into cardiac arrest shortly after I arrived, the staff converged on him like ants to freshly spilled honey. There were screams and shouts and even cheering from the attending doctors and WACs when he was spared from death. It was like a horrific car wreck. I didn't want to watch, but I couldn't help myself from looking.

For the wounded who had been patched up, but who had little chance of survival, Army chaplains rotated from one bed to another, offering prayers, reading the Bible or taking confessions. I was thankful their parents and loved ones back home couldn't see how it all ended for these guys. Each man died alone, without even having his buddies nearby to offer comfort in his last moments of life. And when it came down to it, in this war, the only sense of purpose most of us ever had was to take care of our buddies when they most needed us.

Around 10:00 a.m. I dozed off, and woke a short while later to find issues of *Stars & Stripes*, a military newspaper, and magazines, such as *Time* and *Newsweek*, lying next to me. I began poring through the publications, anxious to learn about what was going on back home. Before I knew it, lunch was being served, including ham, potatoes, salad, and real ice cream.

"Spec 4 Hansen? I'm Captain Williams, your doctor," said a tall, slender, and balding man with horn-rimmed glasses in his forties. "Sorry to interrupt your lunch, but we have to see what's going on with your leg."

With that brief introduction, he pulled away the gauze bandages and let out a shrill whistle, saying, "Jesus Christ, you've got a real mess going on here. To be honest, this is one of the most advanced cases of cellulitis I have run across. Why didn't they send you in earlier?"

"Well, sir, I'm in the 101st Airborne and the CO in my unit only sends guys in for treatment when he sees lots of blood," I responded.

"That seems to be the way it is for all of the airborne divisions, the 82nd, 101st, 173^{rd,} and Special Forces. Everybody wants to say they are the toughest. In my opinion, waiting this long to send you in is inexcusable. This is a preventable condition, if treated properly, but… whatever," he said, as his voice trailed off.

His candor was amazing and refreshingly humorous.

"This is going to hurt a bit and you might not want to look," the doctor said as the shiny metal probe slowly disappeared deep into the swollen tissue midway down my right shin. When the instrument came in contact with the bone, my upper body recoiled from the agonizing pain.

I yelled, "Fucking AAAAAAA!"

Captain Williams peered into the wound through a magnifying glass and was breathing so heavily through his nostrils that I could feel a light breeze on my wound. It gave me the creeps.

"To be perfectly honest, Hansen, this infection looks really nasty. They best thing we can hope for is that it hasn't spread to your tibia. If the shinbone is infected, we will have to remove it. But hey, we won't get into that for now. I'll send this sample off to the lab ASAP and we will get you going on a bunch of penicillin and an IV to get you feeling better. I'll come back in a bit and we'll siphon out the infection. To reduce your discomfort, I'll have one of my prettiest nurses get you some Demerol, and even have her assist with the procedure. How's that sound?"

Before I could respond, he had turned around to the guy next to me, who was wheezing loudly.

After finishing my lunch, I dozed off again, and awoke to the sensation of a warm, silky smooth hand on my left shoulder. I turned over to see a young nurse with alabaster skin, blond hair and a sweet smile. Her hand lingered on my bare skin for a moment. I tingled all over. It had been seven months since I had been touched by a woman.

I was mesmerized.

"Mr. Hansen, my name is Linda, and I need to take your temperature." She leaned forward, shook the thermometer, and placed it in my mouth.

The scent of Ivory Soap and Jergen's Lotion drifted past my nose. She was an honest-to-goodness, real American woman.

Holding a large syringe in her right hand, Linda said, "Mr. Hansen, this is the first in a series of 18 shots over several days I need to give you. I hope you don't mind, but they all have to go in your rear."

"You know, Linda, you can give me as many shots in the butt as you want."

Not acknowledging my comment, she said, "Now, if you just turn on your right side, we can get started." I followed her instructions and pulled up my blue gown, exposing my left cheek. "There we go. See, that wasn't so bad," she said in a soft voice. "Captain Williams and I will be back in a bit to start working on your leg. In the meantime, can I get you anything to make you more comfortable?"

"I'm fine, really fine for now. Thanks, Linda," I said taking in every detail of her face and figure.

Minutes later Captain Williams returned, followed by lovely Linda pushing an aluminum cart filled with medical equipment.

"Spec 4 Hansen, to be candid, this is going to hurt, but it is the quickest way to pull the infection out and get you healthy again," the doctor noted.

As the end of the tube descended into my leg, Linda took my right hand and gave it a squeeze. Immediately, a stream of yellow puss began rising up through the clear plastic tube and into a huge syringe the doctor was holding. The pain was intense and might only have been exceeded if he had smashed my balls with a hammer. My eyes immediately went back to Linda's face in search of comfort, but she was looking down at the floor. Perhaps the gruesome scene was even too much for her.

When the procedure finally ended, I sank back into my pillow and squinted into the glaring light bulb encased in a white metal fixture directly above my head. As the Demoral began to finally ease the throbbing pain, I considered my plight. What if my tibia *was* infected? Maybe they would have to amputate my lower leg? But then I would survive the war and could go home. Perhaps it wasn't such a bad tradeoff. Was I that desperate?

At this moment, it seemed so.

September 25, 1968

LSD is a drug.
LBJ is a dope.
Vietnam is a bad trip.

Hi Sweets,
After 18 shots, they are finally giving me pills—is my butt ever sore!! I should leave here in a few days, hopefully. I am getting bored as hell, but I hate to go back on the line.

God, am I ever in a romantic mood lately. I keep reading these books, looking at your pictures, and thinking about you so much. Never before have I had the time to think about you as I've had in the past week or so. I just lay in bed thinking about kissing you and touching you all over. Your body was always so inviting and cozy to be with on cold nights. I remember every little thing that used to make you react and the caresses you gave me in return. Thank God we have less than 5 months to go now and we can again love each other with even more meaning than we ever had before.

Looking back at the past 7 months, Karen, I know that I'm a much better person. I only hope that I can be a more considerate mate to you than I was before. I've seen so much over here that will stay with me for the rest of my life. It's a constant reminder how lucky I am to have a woman like you to become my wife.

God Bless You.
Love, Jim

Author recovering at the 95th Evac Hospital, Da Nang

October 4, 1968

This is the first time since I've been in this lousy country that I've been able to actually think about this war. I think I've changed so much and at the same time feel like it is mostly to the good. At least I know exactly what is going on over here and will be able to adapt what I've learned to my future as a husband, father, and businessman.

First Reflections

Ghostly images of their faces came into focus for a few seconds and then vanished, one after another, as I rested in my hospital bed late one evening. Dorch, Hayner, Wall, Brehm, Dunlap, Mosley, Ptak, Evans, Purdue, Lopez… Christ, how many guys had been killed since I joined Charlie Company last March? How many more would die in the months ahead?

After two weeks out of the "boonies", I was regaining my sense of feeling… or more specifically, the ability to feel deeply again about things that mattered most in life. Nearly nonstop combat for months had methodically shut down my emotions without me even realizing it. Maybe it was a defense mechanism to protect me from going off the deep end? I had no idea. But the sensation for the past two weeks was as if my entire body was thawing out. Feeling was returning first to my extremities, and eventually all the way to my very core. Sometimes the process brought pain and I ached all over. Yet with each passing day, I felt more focused and able to put things in perspective.

Earlier in the day, I realized people were the most important factor in my ability to survive the war and I was deeply grateful to each one. My buddies came first to mind, because they were the reason I was still alive. They had saved my life more times than I could count. Karen was a close second, because seeing her again was what I lived for every time I hit rock bottom. My family and friends provided comfort at many levels, especially the weekly care packages full of goodies, fresh cigarettes, and newspapers sent by my mother.

This evening, however, I was thinking about the importance of people in a very different way. I was experiencing an enormous sense of loss.

Maybe thirty fucking buddies gone, and counting…

Back home, this would be as if one of your best friends was killed *in front of you* every week. In the most horrific manner imaginable. For seven consecutive months—and with no end in sight.

How does one come to terms with the collective weight of human loss? Can it be rationalized in some fashion? Was this war, or any war, ever worth this kind of sacrifice?

In turn, I had killed the enemy as well, taking the lives of perhaps eight VC/NVA soldiers. There could have been more during the confusion of firefights. What must my victims' family and friends be going through as they learned about their losses? What kind of hell had I created for them?

Then there were the lives of Vietnamese civilians. I had witnessed perhaps one hundred or more perish. How many was I responsible for? There was no way to know for sure. The dead and wounded children always hit me the hardest. I could never get their images out of my head.

No wonder I had gone numb at times.

If only I could escape from this insane war. I hoped and prayed I could go home now and see Karen's beaming smile across the tarmac after we landed. I would run over, sweep her into my arms, kiss her deeply, inhale the distinctive scent of her neck, feel the warmth of her skin, and tell her I love her, knowing at long last that everything was just fine.

I would turn and hug my mother, dad, sisters and friends. Mom would say, as she always did when I had been away, "Welcome home, Sonny! Are you ready for some fried chicken and potato salad?"

Then, deep down, I would know the war was *really* over for me.

October 6, 1968

Dearest Karen,
Today is truly a beautiful day in Da Nang. The sun has come out, there's a light breeze and the temperature is 86 degrees. From the hill outside my ward I can see the South China Sea with Vietnamese junks and Navy ships sailing across the bay. It's really a picture almost too perfect for this country, if that makes sense. I only wish I could stay here until my DEROS.
We could have such a happy life on an island that looks like this view. I can hardly wait for our honeymoon—just to be alone with you and not a care in the world except pleasing you.

In love and lonely,
James

Author graduating from Basic Training, Ft. Lewis, WA.

October 11, 1968

Chopper assault called off this morning because we staged a protest. The weather was terrible with low clouds and pouring rain. The mission was to sweep the same area we had done three times before. It was completely insane. General Zais actually visited us later on, listened to our concerns and changed the mission.

Peace Brother

We'd fucking had it. Squad-by-squad, platoon-by-platoon, every grunt in Charlie Company placed their rifles, machine guns, grenade launchers, and light anti-tank weapons in a cone-shaped pile as our officers watched in disbelief. We formed a circle around the mountain of weapons and sat down in the pouring rain, refusing to move.

Two days earlier, on October 9th, I was discharged from the hospital in Da Nang. I was back in Sally by noon. Before the end of the day, a chopper had taken me to the mountains, about four clicks east of T-Bone, where I rejoined second platoon.

I was back in the shit.

"Hansen, where in the fuck have you been? Thought we might never see you again," Sgt. Sierra said with a wry smile on his face.

"Well, I was hoping they would just cut off my lower right leg so *you* wouldn't see me again, but I wasn't that lucky," I responded with a laugh, handing him a pack of Winstons.

"Thanks man, I just ran out. You know, you're just in time for another fucking ambush. We're pulling one on the trail way below here, where it meets the creek. You might remember it," Sierra said with a hint of sarcasm.

"Jesus, how many fucking times have we been to that same spot? It's probably five hundred meters down to the bottom of the trail and then we gotta hike back up in the morning. And it seems like every damn time we run in to some shit," I added.

"Yeah, I know, I know. Command has its head up its ass as usual. We gotta start heading down there within the hour. See you in a few," Sierra said. He bent down to open up his rucksack and pulled out some letters to read.

The ambush was a bust and the trail remained quiet through the night. But we did do battle, in the nonstop rain—battle with thousands of land leeches looking for higher ground. Like an insect version of the D-Day invasion, leeches the size of two-inch twigs marched out of the water under the cover of darkness and up our boots. Then they somehow crawled inside our pant legs, despite the fact our boots were bloused (tucked in). We could only detect their movement by an occasional creepy tickling sensation.

Once the little critters found tender areas of skin such as armpits, crotches, and necks, they painlessly sucked our blood. When their bodies became bloated, they would fall off, leaving crimson blotches the size of tennis balls on our fatigues—only to be discovered at the first light of day.

Vampires in a war zone.

Second platoon hiked back up the trail at dawn, wheezing by the time we reached the top at 7:00 a.m. While eating LRRP rations for breakfast (freeze-dried food requiring hot water, to enhance the culinary experience), we learned more bad news.

"Command says they want us to head up that peak over there," Lt. Anderson said. He pointed north to a massive green form flanked by steep slopes on all visible sides. It loomed above the valley like an enormous dollop of mint green ice cream.

"No fucking way," I said in a low voice to Sierra. "What is the point? This is just stupid beyond words."

"That's one thing we can all fucking agree on," Sierra whispered.

Our saturated equipment must have weighed over seventy-pounds, it seemed, as we started up the mountain. If that wasn't bad enough, we did battle with "buggy whip" type bushes that constantly slapped us in the face, got snarled on the aluminum frame of our rucksacks, and just drove us nuts. Muddy conditions, the entire way up, created unsure footing. It was just a matter of time before every guy in the company fell face first into the red gunk. Six grueling hours later, we reached the summit and started digging in for the night.

With each shovel full of earth, I thought about how many buddies had been killed since I joined Charlie Company last March. Sitting down on the pile of freshly turned rocks and dirt, I shook my head back and forth in disgust, realizing more than three times that number had no doubt been wounded. The weight of the loss felt like a thousand pounds on my shoulders and I wondered just how much more I could handle.

This mission, like so many in the past, seemed absurd. What was the real purpose? Why did we need to climb the mountain when they could just drop us off at the top from a chopper? Surely, there must have been a compelling reason, but none of our officers had an answer. Our frustration was compounded by the fact that our occupation of the mountaintop would be temporary. Following all of the efforts to "take the hill," we knew we would stay for a day or two and abandon the site. The enemy must have loved this strategy. All they had to do was exercise a little patience and the Americans would eventually move on.

So with the continued absence of mission purpose, the growing number of casualties, coupled with the miserable weather, we decided to take control of our destiny on October 11th. We staged a protest as soon as we returned to Sally. We put peace signs on our helmets, sat down cross-legged in a circle surrounding our pile of weapons, and didn't budge. Since we *were* in a war zone, our demonstration wasn't about peace, not like the ones back home. But we were protesting, nonetheless, what we believed to be pointless missions, creating unnecessary losses in an idiotic war.

About two hours later, the sound of chopper blades from above signaled something was up. The instant the bird landed, an older man bounded from the pilot's seat and walked briskly toward us. The two white stars on the front of his helmet didn't go unnoticed by any of us. Our officers snapped to attention and saluted as we remained on the ground, looking up in disbelief. It was General Zais, Commander of the entire 101st Airborne Division.

"Gentlemen of Charlie Company, 2/501st Infantry, I understand you have a number of concerns. I am here to listen to you and determine how we can work through these issues together," General Zais began. We were shocked that our modest protest could have attracted this much attention and at first we sat there speechless.

The General heard complaints from squad leaders in each of our three platoons, listening intently the entire time. When he finished, Zais promptly aborted the mission. He told us that in the future, Command would revise strategic operations to reduce the number of repetitive missions.

We were elated, though most of us doubted that would ever really happen.

General Zais ordered us into formation and then personally thanked every soldier for their sacrifices. With that, he did an about-face, saluted, and barked "AIRBORNE!"

We all returned his call in unison, shouting back, "AIRBORNE!" Moments later, he jumped back in his chopper, fired up the engine, saluted us through the window, and quickly lifted off.

And we went back to being good soldiers—even feeling like our opinions mattered—at least for today.

October 15, 1968

Dear Family,
I will have to make this a fast letter because we are leaving for the mountains at any time. It depends on the weather. The low clouds are keeping the choppers from landing at our LZ at the moment. One minute it's foggy and the next minute it lifts.

We are headed for a firebase south of Hue called Birmingham. It's been pouring steady for a week and the paddies and rivers are all one now. Things are going OK other than that.

We won't get supplies for 5 days so there will be a gap in the mail again.

I hope you are having a dry and sunny Fall. I will write you again as soon as I can.

Love,
Jim

Author after four months of combat

October 23, 1968

Finally made it to the top of the mountain (over 1,800 meters high), after collapsing on the way up from this horrible case of trench foot. I cried for the first time in months. I doubt whether I've ever been in this much pain in my life. Both my mind and body are a wreck. Thanks to Ogee for helping me keep it together. Off to T-Bone.

Hey Jude

Ogee and I were sitting side-by-side in our two-man foxhole on T-Bone. Our bare feet were propped up on sandbags, catching both the afternoon sun and gentle breeze.

"This is some amazing shit," Ogee said as he took a toke from a joint the size of a small cigar.

"Yeah, I know. We are both totally messed up and we haven't even finished half of this," I said as I took another hit.

"Aren't the Beatles the best ever, man?" Ogee said as "Hey Jude" played from our little AM transistor radio.

"Yep, and along with this fine weed the song takes you away from this goddamn place," I said as he reached over to take the joint from my extended hand.

The previous week had been dominated by endless days of rain with our socks and boots constantly soaked. My case of trench foot had returned with a vengeance and I wasn't alone. The fungus condition was so advanced for fifteen of us that the soles of our feet resembled Feta cheese, with chunks breaking off, revealing raw flesh underneath. To make matters even more disgusting, our feet smelled like rotten fish. Any pressure on them at all created excruciating pain. It was akin to walking on hot crushed glass.

Rather than send us to the hospital, Command got the idea to chopper us up to T-Bone, a recently abandoned LZ. It was a one-of-a-kind South Vietnam mountain resembling Sugar Loaf, the monolithic landmark in Rio de Janeiro. The summit, six hundred meters high, was a narrow barren ridge and perhaps only one hundred meters long, and dotted with several bunkers. Our only orders were to secure the

LZ and leave our feet uncovered in the open air day and night. A chopper dropped us off enough supplies for a week along with a crate of Claymore mines.

In theory, sending us up there had some merit because it freed up space in the overcrowded 95th Evac Hospital in Phu Bai. But the fact was, if the enemy launched an attack, we wouldn't have a chance. Hell, we couldn't even run from the fuckers if we wanted to. We were tin ducks in a carnival shooting gallery.

"Man, I am getting the fucking munchies and all we have for chow are C-rations and LRRP rations. I had some chocolate cookies from home, but they turned to mush in the wet and I tossed them," I said.

"If we only had ketchup or mustard or anything to add flavor to this sorry excuse for beef stew," Ogee said. "What if we have a few more hits and concentrate really hard on a bottle of Heinz 57? Then, maybe we might be able to taste it in the stew?"

"You are really stoned, man, but you know it just might be worth a try," I said as I relit the mammoth joint. "On second thought, let me call around to the other bunkers and see if somebody has some kind of flavoring. If they don't, then we can give your idea a try."

From our perch we could see the South China Sea shimmering in the sun seventeen kilometers to the east. With the elevated level of THC in our bodies, we also enjoyed the distant B-52 air strikes along the Ho Chi Minh Trail. We stared in wide-eyed awe at the distant multi-colored flashes on the western horizon, punctuated by thunderous explosions that sometimes vibrated our clothing.

"Ogee, turn it up, man. I just love the way this song ends."

In unison, we sang at the top of our lungs, *"Na na na naahna na… hey Jude…"*

October 27, 1968

Dear Karen,
Command finally sent a bunch of us over to T-Bone to get rid of our persistent trench foot. We are spending a week on our butts in our bare feet. After four days it seems to be working.

With lots of time to think, I realized today that all I have been living on lately is memories of you. After eight months over here in this shit hole, sometimes I can't even imagine what it would be like to hear your voice again or see you in the flesh. It really gets me down, so I pray each night that our relationship will hang on for four more months.

It seems, by your letters lately, that you have withdrawn into a shell—maybe to protect yourself? What can I do? All I ask is that you keep the faith and try to pull yourself out of that shell—even a little bit.

When I do get home I know exactly what I will find: the only girl that has ever given me true love; the girl that has guided me towards God; and the girl that often needs help and is never afraid to ask me for it.

I feel deep inside that each day, each hour and each minute when we are back together, our relationship will eventually return to what it was before I left. We just both need to BELIEVE in each other no matter the challenges.

To be honest, things here have been the toughest ever. I nearly had a complete breakdown after five straight days of combat and dealing with severe foot pain. At times, I feel I have reached my limit on what I can endure. I need your support more than ever. Please don't pull back any more.

Somehow, someway I am going to survive this fucking war and come home to you. God bless you and hang in there. I know we can do this.

I love you—I'm sure.

James

Countryside following extensive bombing including Napalm

A Sense of Hope

November 4, 1968

Left at 5:50 in the afternoon and it was so good to look back at the coastline of Nam fading into the distance for once.

Heaven

Giddy with excitement, I boarded a Pan Am airliner at Ton Son Nhut Air Base near Saigon. As we taxied down the runway, I sniffed my right sleeve, winced and shook my head. My summer dress uniform still smelled of mildew despite having it cleaned at the base laundry.

"It doesn't fucking matter, man, my clothes stink too," said Mike, a guy from Phoenix sitting next to me. "We'll just buy some new stuff when we get to Sydney."

I agreed. All that mattered now was getting out of Vietnam as fast as possible and flying down to Sydney for six nights and seven days of partying.

As anxious as I was to leave Vietnam, it seemed like eternity before the jet gained enough ground speed to lift off. When it did, a collective roar of approval filled the cabin. As the plane gained altitude and turned southwest towards the equator, I settled back in my seat, pulled out the latest issue of Playboy magazine (a monthly gift from my Mom). I went straight for the centerfold and tried to put the war behind me.

We touched down at 2:00 a.m. in Darwin, a city in the "Top End," as Australians refer to the northern coastal region. "Seems weird that we are stopping here for fuel; you'd think we could easily make it all the way to Sydney," Mike pondered.

"Yeah, man, it's kinda odd, now that you mention it."

The sound of aerosol cans spraying an acrid smelling disinfectant in the cabin announced there was another purpose to our stop. Three uniformed Australian customs officers, wearing gas masks and armed with a can in each hand, methodically fogged up every conceivable space in the aircraft. It was like the CS gas chamber exercise back in Basic Training at Fort Lewis, Washington, where young draftees were forced to breathe tear gas without protective masks so that we could "understand what it felt like," according to our drill sergeant. Now, we were being gassed because we were an apparent threat to society.

With our eyes tearing up and gasping for breath, we were then herded out of the plane and down to the tarmac like Australian sheep. One by one, they instructed us to walk slowly over mats saturated with another disinfectant that oozed up over the soles of our shoes.

Just how contaminated were we from having served in Vietnam? We weren't sure and the officers weren't saying.

The final stage of our Australian cleansing exercise included having our duffel bags searched. They were looking for any material deemed "pornographic," including pictures of (God forbid) naked women and paperbacks with lurid stories of love and lust. I felt like crying when my new Playboy was confiscated. Who knew such things could be a threat to society?

Within an hour or so we were finally on our way—one hundred eighty American soldiers certified to be wholesome and pure by the Australian government.

The sun rose over Sydney just as our Boeing 707 made its final approach. From the air everything appeared so organized. It was a perfect street grid with huge expanses of parks separating residential neighborhoods from commercial centers, wrapped neatly around a picturesque harbor. In the distance I could see pristine beaches with white sand extending for miles. It looked a bit surreal to me—no rockets or bombs exploding, no napalm drops vaporizing the countryside, just people living peacefully in a tranquil setting. I couldn't quite fathom it.

The fresh and distinctive scent of Sydney filled my senses as I squinted into the rising sun and took a deep breath before making my way down the aircraft stairway. What a contrast to the tropical smell of Vietnam, which was dominated by a variety of things in a constant state of decay.

After a quick customs check, we boarded buses for the Chevron Hotel in Kings Cross. (What could possibly be left in our possession to confiscate?) Along the way every guy had his face pressed to the window. We were all mesmerized by the scene playing out in the street. Everything and everyone looked so clean and freshly washed. Nicely dressed businessmen were hurrying to work. London-style taxis darted back and forth. But in the maze of the rush hour traffic, the thing that caught every guy's full attention were the girls in miniskirts—they were strutting around everywhere we looked.

They were the frosting on Sydney's cake.

One hundred and eighty GIs sat cross-legged on the lobby floor of the Chevron Hotel on Lander Street, listening to an Australian government official explain the "dos" and "don'ts," ranging from public drunkenness to drug use to avoiding VD. He was dead serious, and you could tell he had given the speech a thousand times before. But what he didn't know was the real show, which was unfolding directly behind him on the spiral staircase.

With each graceful and measured step, just a little more of her marvelous legs were revealed as she ascended the staircase. They must have been six feet long. By the time she reached the top step, wearing the shortest mini skirt in the Southern Hemisphere, we were convinced we could see a hint of her panties. Were they pink? Were they yellow? None of us knew for sure, but we were *certain* we caught a glimpse of them. Before she disappeared from view, she turned, looked down at us, and winked. My God, it had been way too long since any of us had seen a *real looker*—and now here was one showing off her stuff. Had we all died and gone to heaven?

It was boner city!

November 6, 1968

Dear Karen,
I arrived in Sydney at 6:00 a.m. yesterday and I just love it. The temperature is only 75 and it is so comfortable. I love the people. They are so sincere and hospitable. They would give you their last dollar if you needed it—really different than in the U.S.!

The city has a population of about 3 million and resembles San Francisco with a beautiful harbor and sandy beaches. I wish you were here so we could enjoy it together.

The nightlife here in the Kings Cross area is wild and the kids stay out very late. They have everything for the servicemen you could imagine!

I wish I could be here with you!

Love and Kisses,
James

Sydney Harbor and new Opera House

November 6, 1968

Went to the Whiskey A Go-Go last night and really enjoyed living like a human again. Met a girl who has lived here for a year and she showed me all around the city today. I saw several areas that I would never have seen otherwise. Will go back to the Whiskey again tonight.

Brenda

Motown music blasted from the elevated speakers as we danced on a parquet floor. Bikini clad girls ground their hips back and forth in cages illuminated by an array of colorful flashing lights. It was the Whiskey a Go-Go club at full tilt on Williams Street, half way between the heart of Kings Cross and Hyde Park.

Too many whiskey sours had left my head spinning, so I tried to ward off the buzz by dancing with as many girls as I could find. Sweat was forming on my brow and my new blue shirt was starting to stick to my back, but I was savoring every minute of my first night out in Sydney. Hopefully, the BRUT cologne I wore would help mask my manly scent, should my deodorant fail.

Through the glare of lights and the smoke filled cavernous room, I spotted her. She stood out from the rest of the mini-skirted girls crowding around the perimeter of the dance floor. It was her long, thick dark hair contrasted against her white blouse that first caught my eye. Looking closer, I noticed her smile beaming across the room. Our eyes met and she smiled even wider—not in a flirtatious way, just a pleasant grin, like the wholesome girls back home.

"G'day, I'm Brenda," she said in a heavy Australian accent as she extended her hand to meet mine.

"I'm Jim," I said leaning down close to her ear in order to be heard over the thumping music. "Can I buy you a drink? Maybe it will be a bit quieter over by the bar," I added before she could respond. Brenda nodded in agreement, I grasped her hand and we began maneuvering through a sea of rowdy GIs sprinkled with a dusting of Australian beauties all moving to the pulsating beat. The sensation of her hand in mine was magical. Endorphins rushed through my body. My heart was pounding. I never wanted to let go.

The bar was jammed and the noise level was just the same, if not worse, than the dance floor about ten meters away. Eventually a barmaid slid over a couple of rum and cokes. The instant after I handed Brenda the glass, a girl bumped her from behind and the contents spilled down her sheer white blouse, revealing amazing breasts encased in a pink lace bra. I was fixated on them. When I refocused, I grabbed a towel from the bar and offered to dab up the moisture. Giving me a knowing look, she took the towel, quickly wiped the sticky contents off the blouse as best she could and suggested we leave and look for somewhere to eat.

"There's a place called Mama Marta's Pizza just two blocks up the street that serves some great *tucker*. Does that sound good?" Brenda offered as we emerged from the club.

"Tucker...?" I questioned.

"You know, food!"

"Oh, that sounds perfect; I haven't had pizza since I left home," I replied.

"What part of the States you from, Jim?" Brenda said as we held hands walking down Williams Street.

"The West—Washington State, but I grew up on its southern border, along the Columbia River, close to Portland, Oregon. How about you?"

"Near Alice Springs—that's in the Outback, in the dead center of the country. It's a thousand miles from nowhere."

"Seriously? Alice Springs?"

"You've heard of it?" Brenda responded in disbelief.

"Yeah, I am a geographer at heart, and I always thought it would be a neat place to visit since it is so far from any other city. Isn't it the most remote city of its size in the world?"

"So it's said. I hated the isolation. It was a *no-hoper* for me—there's no jobs, no social life for young people. On top of that, everyone's an *ocker*!"

"A what...?"

"You know, people who lack sophistication. Some folks in Sydney consider Alice Springs to be a *whoop whoop*—a place that is so unimportant they don't even call the city by its name. On top of that, people here tease me about my slang, because it's different than Sydney. But it just goes hand-in-hand with growing up in the Outback. It's part of who I am."

The Righteous Brother's "Unchained Melody" played as we entered the pizza place. It was a bit loud, but compared to the "Whiskey" it was quiet. As we settled into a booth facing one another, she continued her thought, "I moved here about a year ago. I love Kings Cross—there's so much going on, never a dull moment, and the night life is non-stop."

I listened to her for a while without responding. Her accent was so endearing and the slang was a riot to hear and translate. The bright lights in the restaurant made it possible for me to study her face for the first time. What a beauty. Her large deep brown eyes complemented her tanned face outlined in thick black hair that extended almost down to her little waist. A five foot six, she was the complete package in my mind. I just couldn't get enough of her.

"My blouse is a bloody mess. All I can smell is rum and coke." With that, she sprayed some perfume on each side of her neck, filling the booth with a scent of gardenia, my favorite.

For that moment, the war—and Karen—were the furthest things from my mind.

I reached over, took both of her hands in mine to assure her she still looked fantastic despite the spots on her blouse. Squeezing my hands in return she looked up and said, "Well Jim Hansen from Washington State, welcome to the Land Down Under. Now, what kind of pizza do you want?"

While the sun-dried tomato and sausage pizza tasted wonderful, I was far more consumed by the novelty of having a conversation with this nineteen-year old girl. Feeling the warmth of her hands, the scent of her perfume and watching the excitement in her eyes, made me feel better than any pot I had ever smoked in Vietnam. I almost felt weightless.

After I walked her back to her apartment, I gave her a kiss goodnight. It was everything a first kiss should be, warm, tender and euphoric. We parted slightly, kissed again and the sensation was even more intense. It was almost more than I could handle, so I squeezed her hands and asked if I could see her the next day.

"I would love to see you again. How would you like to see some more of Sydney?" Brenda said. Before I could respond she added, "I will meet you at your hotel… say around ten?"

I was down in the lobby a few minutes early the following morning and was delighted to see her walk through the door moments later. Following a long hug and a kiss, Brenda said, "Hey, it's bloody beautiful out. How 'bout walking down to the bay and taking the ferry over to the Taronga Park Zoo? It's a scenic ride and you can get great views of the city over and back."

"Sounds good to me!" I quickly said, and we were out the door, walking hand in hand down the street like old friends.

We snuggled on a bench near the bow of the ferry. Brenda pointed out all of the key landmarks, including the Sydney Opera House under construction with its distinctive layered white roof. While I was listening to every detail about the sights of Sydney, I found myself distracted. Little things, like the way the wind blew her long black hair in waves over her shoulder, or how her lips formed words when she talked, consumed me. But my attraction to her wasn't just physical. I was impressed with her maturity. She had a timeless presence about her. She frequently offered insight about life from a perspective well beyond her nineteen years. I couldn't have been more intrigued.

Brenda also understood I was aching to experience some semblance of a normal life. To that end, she created a list of places we could visit over the next five days when she wasn't working her part-time shift at the Contemporary Record store. We took a tour of the harbor, sunbathed on the white sands of Bondi Beach, got wasted at the Texas Tavern and had dinner at Bourbon and Beefsteak. *Life was good.*

To give me a taste of life outside of Sydney, we took a train to nearby Wollongong and listened to her favorite rock band. We hung out with her friends and spent much of the evening discussing Australia's role in the war. Given their close proximity to Southeast Asia, the government justified sending troops to the front lines in Vietnam, based on the "Domino Theory"—the premise that if an Asian country like Vietnam fell to the Communists, Malaysia, Indonesia, the Philippines and Australia wouldn't be far behind. I thought it was idiotic. But opinions were mixed in this crowd of late teens and early twenties. Many said the Aussies had no business in Vietnam, especially with the increasing number of casualties.

The conversation eventually changed to contrasts between the American and Australian lifestyles. We kidded each other back and forth for some time about why Americans seemed so uptight compared to the easy going Aussies, who never took anything too seriously. But two of the local guys were becoming agitated. For one thing, they resented GIs for dating "their girls," as they put it.

In addition, they didn't appreciate me questioning their social customs such as pubs that only allowed women to be served ale through a portal on the street while the men sat inside. I thought my teasing remarks were all in jest, but one of the guys was drunk and took my words as a insult.

"It's the fuck'n way it is here, soldier. So don't go put'n ideas in our girl's heads. Me an' me mates need the pubs to ourselves. If our chicks really want to be at the pub, they fuck'n well have to stand on the street. Got a problem with that?" The lanky fellow, easily over six feet tall, pointed at me with his glass, beer sloshing out in every direction.

"Well, I just see it as disrespectful to women, that's all," I said as I turned toward Brenda and gave her a nod.

I never saw the fist that smashed the right side of my face. Nor did I see the second one that sent me flying backward onto the floor. I didn't have the urge to counter his blows. *Just what I needed, more violence*—the very thing I so desperately wanted to escape from on my R&R.

Brenda whisked me out of the club and down to the train station before the situation worsened. She took ice from a cup of a Coke, created a cold press with a napkin that I held to my face all the way back to Sydney.

As I waited the following day for her work shift to end, I walked down to the harbor and tried to put things in perspective. It occurred to me that Brenda and I had become a couple. Things had gone from "I" to "we" and it felt comfortably familiar—just like it had been with Karen. I loved being with her no matter what we were doing. It was exciting to hear a woman's point of view, after being with no one but men for so long. She always had an interesting take on virtually any topic that came up, so much like Karen. In an odd sort of way, it was as if Brenda had become my surrogate fiancée. Everything was feeling like it once did before the war. There was no end to how much of this new life, however temporary, I could absorb.

Our affection for one another increased this feeling of familiarity even further. We stood next to the bed in my hotel room later than evening, fully clothed, kissing and nuzzling. She gave me the most amazing French kiss I could have every imagined. I felt my spine melt and we rolled slowly down on the bed together with our arms and legs interlocked. After several minutes, we stopped kissing and just held one another. Remaining motionless and face-to-face, we inhaled each other's breath slowly—in and out—in the same rhythm. The sensation was so intense we remained in that position for the longest time.

Another object of my affection was her remarkable breasts, the size of large grapefruits and perfectly shaped. Kissing and caressing them overwhelmed me at times. I just couldn't get enough of them. In this moment, they were all that I needed.

In the days that followed, we never did make love, despite spending hours naked in bed. It was akin to eating fresh rhubarb pie from the garden back home. Sometimes the filling and homemade crust was so satisfying, that a dollop of vanilla ice cream on top just didn't seem that important.

While Brenda was very responsive, she seemed content not to take things to another level. She also had an aura of innocence about her that I deeply respected. Having sex with her crossed my mind frequently, but it didn't seem like something we *had* to do to be mutually satisfied.

I headed down to the harbor on my last full day in Sydney while I waited for Brenda to get off work. Sitting at the water's edge, smelling the salt air and listening to the sounds of shore birds flying by, I reflected on the past five days. It had been a heavenly experience at so many levels, and with every passing day I felt more alive and vibrant. The numbness that had once enveloped my body was now gone.

My rediscovered emotions, however, such as the ability to give and receive affection from a woman, or to experience what it was like to live in a peaceful society, had an unexpected downside. While I could now visualize what things would be like when I returned to the States, and while I felt euphoric when dreaming about my future, I was freshly jolted by the realization that *everything* I had to live for was at risk.

In less than two days I'd be back in the shit.

Could I survive three more months of combat? Was there a realistic chance—given that one out of every two guys in Charlie Company had either been killed or wounded so far? Who was I kidding? I might not make it another week if I wasn't careful *and* lucky.

I tried to put those troubling thoughts out of my mind on my way back to the hotel by visiting a number of shops and buying things for Karen, my family, and of course, Brenda.

"G'day! How sweet! You bought me a prezzy," Brenda said. I handed her a wrapped package when I walked into the Contemporary Record shop. "Here," she said as she gave it back to me. "Let me go wash up. I will be ready to take off in a few minutes and then I will open it up."

As we walked down Richards Street arm-in-arm, she tied the new scarf around her neck and gave me a kiss on the cheek. "Thanks, James! This is lovely, and you are so thoughtful. What do you say we head down to Pink Pussycat and I buy you a drink?"

"Sounds good to me," I said. We were both feeling a bit subdued for the first time in our five-day relationship. The end of our magical ride was hours away.

By midnight, we had both had enough of the Kings Cross club scene and we headed back to my hotel for some solitude. Lying on the bed together for several minutes in silence, Brenda was the first to speak. "I knew from the first night when we met at the 'Whiskey' and went out afterward for pizza, that our time together would be temporary. I also knew if I wanted to protect myself from getting hurt, I should keep my distance and not get too close to you. I have been through this with some other guys and have found it's best to always hold back."

She paused, sighed, and then went on, "That seemed to work at first, but by the second day I knew I couldn't control my emotions. You didn't know it, but I almost split at that point. Now it's too late. No matter how hard I try to keep some distance, you've touched my heart. I care for you so much, and I just can't bear to say goodbye..." her words trailed off as she began crying in my arms.

"Brenda, sweet Brenda, I feel the same. You are an incredibly bright and beautiful girl. You've helped me in so many ways. You made it possible for me to experience real emotion—to have normal feelings again. Our time together has been so special. I can't begin to thank you for being so patient and understanding. On top of that, you even rescued my ass from a fight that night in Wollongong."

Following a quick laugh, she started crying again.

I said, "Like you, I initially tried to distance myself from you, knowing our time together would end way too soon. But my feelings got away from me. I ache inside when I'm not with you. I never want to let you go."

With our arms and legs completely entwined on the bed, we cried for the longest time and eventually dozed off.

Around 3:00 a.m., my roommate, Joe Thompson, burst through the door with a bottle of champagne in one hand and two glasses in the other—drunk out of his mind. Brenda and I grabbed the sheets in unison and pulled them up to our necks. I hadn't seen him for five days. His sudden intrusion turned out to be very timely. Up to this point neither of us had been able to take the initiative to say goodbye and now we both wanted to get the hell out of the room and let him party on his own.

After calling a cab, we left Joe and walked silently down to the lobby holding each other tightly. Neither of us could speak following our final kiss. She climbed into the cab. As it sped away, Brenda turned around and waved through the rear window.

The image of her sad eyes and forced smile would be frozen in my mind for the rest of my life.

At 7:30 a.m. sharp, the airport bus honked its horn several times signaling to every GI in the hotel lobby that their R&R was officially over. On queue, Joe ran out of the elevator with his uniform in complete disarray. We made our way toward the back of the bus and plopped ourselves down on the seats in unison. For the entire forty-five minute ride, Joe and I never exchanged a word.

There was so much to talk about, but neither of us had anything to say.

November 11, 1968

Hi Karen,

I really feel like a bum on my letter-writing lately. I wrote you several days ago and gave it to my buddy Joe to mail, but he forgot.

Well, my visit to Sydney was quite an experience. I went all over the city. I spent the afternoons sightseeing and the nights at the clubs. Each evening I ate very well with steak and wine. I even ran into an old A.I.T. buddy and made some Aussie friends as well. The people couldn't have been any more sincere, friendly, and hospitable.

I hope you like your Christmas present I sent you from Sydney. I sent all of the gifts to my folks and they will forward yours to you. I wasn't quite sure what you would like, but I tried my best.

Now that I've had my taste of life as I once knew it, I really hunger to return to Seattle and you. It's just 117 more days! I am so anxious to see how much we have changed. I still firmly believe we will be just as electric as before—although it may take some time to adapt to each other after a year apart.

I hate to think about going back to Charlie Company and the war. Sydney was a real wake-up call for me. Honestly, I had forgotten what it was like to be in a place that was normal. The thought of being in combat again is just too much.

This whole thing is so fucked up.

I love you,
Jim

Brenda walking towards WWI Memorial, Sydney

November 12, 1968

On the flight from Sydney to Bien Hoa AFB, I was very sad to leave Brenda. I am worried about not making it. My mind seems very weird right now. It almost snapped when I got on the C-130 for Hue.

New Lease on Life

"Get yo' shit on and get out to the fucking chopper pad ASAP!" First Sergeant Jackson bellowed from the door of our headquarters bunker in Camp Sally. "Yo R&R is fucking over and now yo' boys got a war to go'n fight," he added with a demonic chuckle.

As the former boxing champion of Ft. Campbell, Kentucky, "First Sarge" was as fierce looking as any six-foot-five, 250 pound black man could ever be. Picture a taller and meaner looking Mike Tyson, before the facial ink. You did what you were told without the slightest hesitation or there would be instant hell to pay.

Four of us, fresh from our R&R's in places ranging from Bangkok, Tokyo, Honolulu, and Sydney, scrambled out to the pad while still stuffing equipment into our rucksacks. Within minutes, a Huey was hovering overhead, filling the air with blinding red dust. Just as I stepped on the landing rail to hoist myself up onto the floor of the bird, my rucksack was suddenly pulled backward with my body in tow. The impact of slamming down on the ground left me stunned. I looked up through the red dust cloud to see First Sarge staring down at me. "Where in the fuck yo' think yo' going, Hansen?" he yelled over the roar of the rotor blades.

"To the boonies, First Sarge," I replied.

"No yo' ain't! Yo gonna be my supply sergeant."

With his simple declaration, First Sarge gave me a new lease on life.

That evening he called me into his tent, broke open a bottle of Jack Daniels, and poured me two fingers worth into an aluminum canteen cup. "Hansen, yo' probably wondering why I picked yo' over some of the other grunts in Charlie Company."

"Absolutely. I still can't believe it," I said.

"Yeah, well, first of all, yo' been in the boonies for nine months and been through a lotta shit. Yo' paid yo' dues. Yo proved to me yo' a good soldier. Yo' went to college and can type... right?"

I nodded "yes" as I tried to gulp down the whiskey without coughing and making a fool of myself.

"Hansen, them are all of the qualifications yo' need. Yo' a grunt and yo' know the kind of support grunts need to survive in combat. Right? So, if I say yo' got to get them Snickers, or smokes, or fucking dirty magazines, yo' gonna find whatever I say and get em' out on the next supply run. If yo' have to steal shit, it don't fucking matter, but I don't wanna know about it. All that matters is that yo' taking care of our men. If yo' fuck up once, yo' white ass will be back out there in the shit quicker than yo' can say 'First Sarge is the finest soldier in the goddamn Army!' Is that totally fucking clear, Hansen?"

"Yes, First Sarge."

"Now get the fuck out of here before I change my mind," he said as he hoisted the bottle above his head and chugged down several gulps.

The next morning I inventoried all of the existing supplies I knew my buddies would want the most. Then I spent the rest of the day talking to other supply sergeants in the area about potential sources for hard to find items. After I found the key contact to the local black market, a Vietnamese supply worker named "Sam," I bought a bottle of Jack Daniels for five dollars and put it on First Sarge's desk with a "Thank You" note.

Twice a week I made a supply run out to the boonies on a Huey, making sure above all else that the right mailbag went to each platoon. There was nothing more important than the mail to a GI in a war zone. In addition to the items on the manifest, I always tried to bring a surprise like ice-cold Cokes. Anything, no matter how small, to help lift their spirits.

By the third week of November, the enemy stepped up their attacks and supply deliveries became even more risky. On the twenty-seventh, just as our bird touched down on a hilltop six kilometers east of T-Bone, we started taking incoming rounds from snipers on a distant ridgeline. The door gunner closest to me screamed "Motherfucker!" and I looked over to see he had been hit. I dove into the bundle of supply bags as the pilot attempted to make an emergency lift off. As the rounds zinged by, one of them hit a bag of sodas I was straddling causing several cans to explode. With no pain and only cold wetness on my fatigues I knew I was good to go.

When we were airborne and out of range of the snipers, I checked on the door gunner who was moaning above the noise of the chopper blades. His right shoulder was oozing blood. I pushed a compress into the bullet hole and tried to make him as comfortable as possible for our thirty-minute ride back to Camp Sally.

"Thanks, man," he said.

"No problem. You're gonna be fine. I wish I had some morphine, but the best I can offer you right now is a soda. They've gotta be good, they just saved my ass."

I could sense First Sarge might be pleased with my performance as the days passed, but he never let on to it. It wasn't until a few weeks later that I knew for sure. Out the blue he dropped an order form on my desk indicating I was promoted to Sergeant. E-5. As walked out of the bunker, he said, "Don't let this go to yo' fucking head, Hansen."

November 20, 1968

Dear Jean,
It's about time that I wrote you a letter. I must owe you about six by now. Thanks so much for the ginger cookies—they were outta sight! You're the BEST SISTER!

My new supply sergeant job has me running from 5:00 a.m. until 10:00 p.m., but compared to being out in the boonies, I can't even complain. I went from sleeping on the ground with the snakes and bugs to sleeping on a cot in a bunker that's safe and clean. It's kind of weird though because sometimes I feel guilty for not being out there with my buddies. Consequently, I am working harder than ever to find them things that matter, like transistor radio batteries, cigarettes, and candy.

I also have to do lots of stupid paperwork related to replenishing supplies of every imaginable kind. But no matter how tedious it gets, I love using my mind again for something other than trying to kill gooks. The only risks I have now are when I take supplies out to my buddies in the boonies by chopper.

The weather here is finally starting to cool down following the monsoon season—like in the 80's during the day.

Your Loving Brother

Camp Sally hooches and bunkers

January 12, 1969

Took Jeter to LBJ today but had to stay in Camp Eagle because we missed the flight. Six rockets were fired at the base at 2:00 a.m. and some came as close as 30 meters. I'm way too short for this shit.

No, Not That LBJ

"You're fucking hurting me," Jeter screamed as Sgt. Johnson, an MP, squeezed the handcuffs as tight as possible on his wrists while I pinned him to the ground with my right knee.

Jeter was skinny, but a very strong African American, about six feet tall. He was a classic fuckup, but in a different way than Youngblood, whose mere presence on the battlefield put everyone's lives at risk. Jeter, in contrast, was rarely in the boonies with us because he was always in Camp Sally with another "medical" issue. So the only real risk he presented to us was his propensity to steal.

He took anything of marginal value, from our duffel bags locked in storage units to items in our "care packages." If you turned your back on him for a second, your Snickers bar would disappear. When he wasn't stealing from us, he ingested every drug he could get his hands on including pot laced with heroin, or "skag."

"Well, if you fucking relax and stop fighting us, maybe I'll let up on the pressure," Sgt. Johnson said.

"That's right man," I said. "Just behave and we'll make this easier for you. If you don't, we'll really make you fucking miserable."

The enjoyable routine of being the Charlie Company supply Sergeant was broken on the 11th when the First Sergeant told me I had to take Jeter to the Long Binh Jail (LBJ) near Saigon. Between his stealing and drug use, we all had wondered when Command would have enough and court-martial the bastard. It finally happened on January 10th. He was convicted of taking a radio and liquor from the battalion mess sergeant and was sentenced to six months in LBJ. But he wasn't going to go easily.

The only time Jeter didn't try to escape was when we were in the C-130 aircraft and there was no place to go. Otherwise, he tried to run for it twice from our Jeep between Sally and the Phu Bai airport, and again right after we landed down in Tan Son Nhut Air Base near Saigon. The MP and I both had several bruises and scrapes by the time we rolled up to the prison gate in the Jeep.

"Jeter, I think you are fucked, man," Johnson said as he unlocked the handcuffs. I released him to a scary looking prison guard—imagine the Incredible Hulk in jungle fatigues.

"But I never did nothing wrong. I shouldn't be here," Jeter said to the Hulk.

"Yeah, yeah, yeah, that's what all of you motherfuckers say," the Hulk replied.

As I looked past the gate, I could see the place was a total shit hole. This wasn't some holding area, it was a prison in every sense of the word. It was what I imagined San Quentin must have been like. Ironically, life there was probably more hellish than being out in the boonies with us.

"Good luck, man," I said to Jeter as the guard led him toward the processing center. He looked back over his right shoulder, opened his mouth as if to speak, but no words came out. His eyes spoke for him. They were the size of silver dollars.

January 13, 1969

Dear Karen,
I've been in Bien Hoa for two days now, enjoying myself. I had to bring a prisoner down to LBJ (Long Binh Jail) yesterday and will pick up another tomorrow. It's been nice to swim and go to the local clubs for a change.

I hope all is well with you despite your record cold weather. It was 95 degrees here today, but I long for cold weather and snow. This 11month summer is getting old!

I will leave here for home on February 27th, rather than the 26th. There was some sort of mistake. Sigh!

I'm at our 2nd Brigade Headquarters and this place even has TV! You know what's on? COMBAT for Christ's sake! What a bummer!

I love you, honey and will see you real soon.

James

Lt. Santos, Sgt. Eaves, Sgt. Otto, Sgt. Beaty, Sgt. Sierra (R to L)

THE WAY HOME

February 15, 1969

Had a great time down south after we took Jeter to LBJ because Command sent us over to Vung Tau (a former French resort on the South China Sea) to pick up Murphy, who had gone AWOL. The place was amazing. You would never know a war was going on.

The Shortest Short Timer

I was filled with emotion and most of it was fear. It was February 16th and I was on my last supply run from Sally out to Charlie Company. As the Huey descended toward the tiny LZ, a few clicks west of Firebase Lyon, my stomach was churning. The NVA had attacked the night before. The last thing I needed right now was the enemy firing up our chopper. I just wanted to get in and get out in one piece as fast as we could.

"How short are you, man?" Hardin asked as I was dragging the mailbags off the chopper.

"Really short, man. I'm down to seven days and a wake-up," I said.

"No shit? Then you must be the shortest short timer man in Charlie Company," he said.

"Yep, and I couldn't be more nervous. Actually, I'm scared shitless that something is gonna happen and I won't make it back to the World."

"You will, man, and I will be right behind you in twenty-one days and a wake-up," Hardin said with a twinkle in his eyes. "They're sending me to Fort Riley, Kansas for some crazy ass reason."

"No shit?" I said. "Well, how 'bout Ft. Bragg, North Carolina? The fucking Army has me going to the goddamn 82nd Airborne. Here I am a fucking 'leg' and they're sending me to another airborne unit. It was bad enough putting up with all of the airborne bullshit like white side walls (a buzz cut on the temples) here in Nam and now I'm gonna have to put up with the same shit in the States."

The chopper lifted off. It would be returning for me in less than an hour. I scanned the perimeter of the LZ and quickly went around to all of my closest buddies to say goodbye. My heart felt like it weighed a hundred pounds as I gave everyone in second platoon a pack of Camels, a Hershey's bar, and a hug. I tried my best to hold back the tears, but it was no use. By the time I reached the last one, I was a sobbing mess and everyone was giving me shit about crying.

The bond we had between us was as powerful as Super Glue. They were the reason I was alive and vice versa. We had saved each others' ass more times than we could count. So much of what we felt for each other over the past year often went unsaid. It was a level of love for sure, but none of us would have ever used that word for fear of being called a "queer." If anything, our affection was conveyed through our eyes, with just a knowing glace and a nod from time to time. When ever again in life would any one of us feel this profound sense of trust and devotion towards another man?

We all made plans to reconnect back in the States, but I knew it was unlikely I would ever see most of them again. If some weren't killed or wounded in the months ahead, they would probably not be assigned to my new unit. It was the reality of serving in this war.

Unlike WWII and the Korean Conflict, and more recently in Iraq and Afghanistan, your only connection with your unit was the time you were in Vietnam. Most of us arrived and departed individually. You didn't know most of the guys before the war and you probably wouldn't see them afterward. Your relationship with them was temporary. It was akin to serving time. (The exception was when an entire unit was transferred over from a U.S. base. The 2/501st Infantry initially arrived together from Ft. Campbell, Kentucky in 1967.)

The chopper lifted off quickly. Grasping the door handle, I leaned out and waved goodbye. My last memory of Charlie Company, 2/501st infantry, 101st Airborne will always be the image of looking down and seeing a hundred guys giving me the finger.

February 18, 1969

Dearest Family,
This is my final letter from the most messed up country in the world. I can't begin to thank you enough for your support throughout this year. So many times a letter arrived from you that gave me enough will to keep driving on.

I always had more mail from home than nearly anyone else and felt so proud that my family cared that much to write (and send care packages!) so often.

And Jean, your cute little cards and notes were precious and could only have been written by the most wonderful little sister in the world!

God bless you all and I'll see you next week.

Love,
Jim

Huey on air assault mission

February 19, 1969

Tomorrow I will finally begin the departure process from this Godforsaken country, traveling south to Bien Hoa to DEROS. In some ways it seems like a lifetime since I was last home and with Karen, while in other ways, it has gone fast.

I've learned one hell of a lot since last March 1st that I would never have experienced if I had stayed in the States. For this and only this, I am thankful that I was sent over here.

If I can someday manage to forget the bad memories and only capitalize on my experiences, maybe I will be able to achieve true happiness in life. I'm sure the children that Karen and I raise will benefit from the understanding that I have about people.

There's not much more to say other than I'm going back both bitter and happy—and hopefully that bitterness will die with the happiness and love that I will gain.

There's Just One Thing

"Incoming, incoming," someone yelled. We were midway through watching "The Dirty Dozen" outside a bunker adjacent to Tan Son Nhut Airbase. Scrambling in every direction, two hundred G.I.s vanished within seconds just before several one hundred twenty-two millimeter rockets came screaming down. The upside was they missed our bunker. The following morning, we learned the rocket hit the runways.

The NVA chose our last night in Vietnam to attack Tan Son Nhut, something that hadn't happened here for over six months. That next morning, DEROS officials confirmed what we had suspected. No "Freedom Birds" (commercial jets) would fly in or out for at least three days. We could sit on our butts all day, fuming about the delay, or spend the time looking for another way out. After two attempts at asking around, I finally hit pay dirt.

"Sir, any chance you might be headed to Cam Ranh Bay today?" I asked, looking at a tall, burley Warrant Officer standing next to a vintage twin engine DC-3.

"Yep. We're making a mail run out that way in a couple of hours. Given the shorter take off distance for these birds, we'll have just enough runway to get off. Ya'll need a ride?" he said in what sounded like a west Texas accent.

"Yes sir. Nine of us are ready to DEROS, but they say we're stuck here until they fill the pocks in the runways," I replied.

"No problem. We've got plenty of capacity. I'm Warrant Officer Brown," he said as he extended his right hand.

"I'm Sergeant Hansen. Pleased to meet you, sir. Thanks so much for your offer. You have no idea how much this means to us."

"I do, son. I do," he said with a big smile.

When he gave us a hand signal across the tarmac later in the morning, we scrambled on board only to find no seats—just a bunch of multi-colored mailbags and three cables stretched across the gleaming aluminum floor of the fuselage. We tossed our duffel bags along the edges of the floor and waited for his instructions on where to sit.

"Boys, just grab one of them lines when we are taking off and landing and you'll be just fine. Oh, there's just one thing, we gotta make a couple of stops along the way over to Cam Ranh Bay. No big deal," he added with a chuckle.

Sitting side-by-side, cross-legged and three to a row, with the cable extended across our laps, I noticed nearly all of the guys were pretty quiet. Maybe, like me, they were beginning to wonder if hitching a ride on the DC-3 was such a great idea. We were desperate to get home, but as "short timers," none of us wanted to take any additional risks in the process. There was an inherent risk to flying to remote air bases in the middle of nowhere, given how easy it would be for the enemy to fire on a slow moving plane like this.

The first mail stop, less than an hour to the east, was uneventful. We touched down on a large, smooth concrete runway with plenty of room to maneuver. But the second stop required landing on a narrow vintage WWII corrugated steel runway surrounded by dense jungle. From far above, it looked more like a pipeline rather than a real runway, hardly suitable for a plane the size of a DC-3 to land. With palm trees crowding the edges of the tarmac, the small encampment surrounding the airstrip appeared like something out of the film *South Pacific*. We exchanged nervous glances as we descended in the choppy air.

The perfect landing on his first try proved that Warrant Officer Brown was a skillful pilot. The plane bounced along the uneven surface and came to a gentle stop. Everyone began to relax a little after the last mailbag was handed off the ground crew.

Then there was the takeoff. Just as the DC-3 cleared the top of the jungle canopy and reached an altitude of about three hundred meters, the starboard engine began sputtering. Smoke poured out of the exhaust with each "pop" of the engine and the propeller slowed to a stop. We sat in silent disbelief. Only the voices of W.O. Brown and his co-pilot could be heard, as they desperately tried to "feather" the throttle to restart the engine.

The starboard wing dipped, we started to lose altitude and the soldier in the row behind me summed up the moment in four words. "I think we're fucked."

In the precious seconds that followed, we exchanged nervous glances and gripped the cables with white knuckled hands. Hearts pounded. Jaws clenched. Some puked. Others prayed.

Just as we braced for the inevitable crash, the starboard engine sprang back to life with a thunderous explosion followed by a puff of white smoke. The propeller turned into a blur, emitting a high-pitched whine, a sound welcome to our ears. We felt the G-force pull at our bodies, and we knew we were in a steep climb.

In the precious second that followed, we released our cramped hands from the cables. Fists pumped. Soldiers hugged. Some yelled. Others prayed.

February 19, 1969

Karen Ann,
This is my final letter from the land of confusion and conflict where I have been so fortunate to spend this past year.

There is no need for a summary of what has transpired. However, I must say without your letters and your support I never would have made it. I'll never be able to thank you enough for the many darling cards and notes that arrived just as I was about to give up. Many times, your unique thoughts were the only thing that gave me the confidence that was needed to believe our relationship could make it for one very long year.

I firmly believe you had the toughest end to pull between the two of us—as far as our relationship goes—and you really came through with flying colors. You were put to the supreme test of faithfulness and devotion and more than passed. I've often wondered if I were in your place if I could have done the same. I have more confidence in you for that alone that I ever though possible. What can I say except that I Love You Karen!

God bless you and I'll see you next week.

Always,
James

A Shau Valley under clouds

Kissing the Tarmac

We were going home. They were going to Hell.

We scrambled to climb aboard our Freedom Bird at dawn on February 27, 1969, just as a planeload of GIs from the States arrived at the adjacent gate. We screamed and shouted with glee as we bounded up the steps. They left the plane and descended the stairs in wide-eyed silence.

As I settled into my seat, I looked up to see a lanky, tanned soldier plop himself down next to me with a long drawn out sigh.

"I just can't believe it, man. We are getting the fuck out of this place today," he said. "I never thought it would happen. I shoulda been killed many times, but..."

"I'm with you, man. I'm with you," I said. "I don't know how I survived this goddamn war either, but here we are... going back to the World. My name is Hansen," I said.

"I'm Johnson... from Seattle," he said as he shook my hand.

"No shit? I'm from Washington, too. It's a little town called Woodland down near Mt. St. Helens."

"Well, this is just too much. I think we need to celebrate a little," he said with a smirk on his face. He reached into the breast pocket of his uniform and producing a quarter-sized brown chip. "Primo hash from my brother in Morocco, man," Johnson said. "A little bit will go a long way. Just take a tiny bite and chew it slowly."

"Fucking A," I said. I put it up to my nose, inhaled the pungent odor, and took a small bite.

We were washing the hash down with some water as the Boeing 707 lifted off and headed for Japan to fuel up before crossing the Pacific. As we looked back through the cabin window at Cam Ranh Bay disappearing into the morning haze, we gave it the finger in unison and settled back in our seats for the trip of our lives.

"What in the Hell are you guys on?" the Master Sergeant in the row in front of us yelled over the top of his seat.

"Nothing, Sarge, we're just excited about going back to the World," I replied.

"Don't lie to me, soldier. You're on something," he barked. "You two have been fucking talking nonstop for the last hour and it's driving me fucking crazy. Couldn't you just shut up for awhile?"

"Sorry, Sarge, we will do our best," Johnson replied with a huge grin on his face.

Our amazing drug trip was interrupted a few hours later when a baritone voice announced over the intercom, "This is your captain speaking. Boys, we should be on the ground at Yokoto Air Base in about thirty minutes. They're reporting blowing snow with a visibility of about one mile. Imagine that!"

As Johnson and I stumbled towards the open door, totally stoned, we looked at each other in collective disbelief as frigid air rapidly replaced the warm, stuffy atmosphere in the cabin. A moment later we stepped out into the cold and were mesmerized by the giant snowflakes hitting our faces.

"See how many you can catch in your mouth, Johnson," I said.

"You're on, man, but I'm tripping out… it's hard to focus on just one at a time. There's just way too many coming at me, way too fast."

Back in the plane after a thirty-minute stop, I grabbed a blanket to ward off the chill and thought about what awaited me at home. After 365 days of waiting, I would finally be with Karen once again. I knew I was a different man in so many ways. How would she react? Would she still love me?

And what about changes in her? She had been actively involved in peace protests at the University of Washington. Her best friend Paulette had joined the Students For a Democratic Society (SDS). And here I was, a Sergeant in the Army, returning from the very war they were protesting. Clearly, I had no idea what I was in for.

Eight hours and many Snickers bars later, we began our descent. Who knew the tarmac of McCord Air Force Base in Tacoma, Washington could look so inviting? From high above, the diagonal landing strips were illuminated by the late day sun, creating a golden sheen. Fatigue from not sleeping for the entire flight was easily overcome with the euphoria of returning home. We weren't alone. When the wheels touched down and the tires responded with a couple of chirps, the cabin was filled with one hundred seventy-five GIs whooping it up.

As I took the last few steps down the stairway and dropped to my knees, I was drawn to the dark gray mass of concrete and asphalt. The petroleum taste of the tarmac on my lips had a sweetness to it that I savored in the moment. This was all the proof I needed that it wasn't a dream.

I had survived the war. I was back in the World.

My spirits were dampened a bit after clearing customs when I saw hopelessly long lines in front of several pay phone booths. Everyone was calling home. Rather than wait an hour or more, I took a shuttle bus over to nearby Madigan Hospital to make my call and see my hometown buddy Tom Karnis, who was recovering from an ambush where he lost his left lung. He was serving as an infantryman with the First Air Cavalry Division and was lucky to have lived. He had been in the hospital for over a month and had no idea I was coming to visit.

But first I had to make my call. I jumped out of the shuttle before it came to a complete stop and sprinted toward the phone booths.

"Would you accept a collect call from James Hansen?" the operator asked my mother.

"Oh, thank God, he's finally home," she responded without ever saying "yes."

"Hi Mom," I said casually. "Do you have any fried chicken and potato salad?"

"Sonny, it's you. You made it back alive," Mom kept saying over and over between sobs.

Opening page of The Little Red Notebook

Home

I had just finished inhaling my second helping of Mom's fried chicken and potato salad when I looked up and saw the 1965 blue metallic Chevy SS Malibu pull into the driveway. Karen had just completed the two and half hour drive from her parent's home in Yakima following my call to her when I arrived at McChord Air Force Base. To save some precious time, she drove straight to Woodland.

"Hansee!" she screamed as the car door swung open into my left knee. Stumbling around the sharp edge of the door, our bodies met just as she rose to her feet.

"Karen," I responded as I picked her four foot, ten inch frame, kissed her and gave her a never ending hug. The taste of her lips, smell of her neck and the natural fit of our bodies was sensational. It reduced both of us to tears. My senses were on overload. I had forgotten what it was like to feel this level of intensity. I missed her more than ever and never wanted to let go of her trembling body.

"It's finally over, Honey. We'll never be apart again," I said nuzzling her thick mane of waist-length auburn hair.

"I can't believe you are really home," she said over and over as we hugged and kissed for several minutes.

After spending the next couple of hours visiting with Mom, Dad, and my little sister Jeanie, Karen and I headed out to the Airstream trailer parked in my parents' oversized garage to get physically reacquainted. It was the perfect cozy getaway. We had all of the privacy we needed—except when my Dad walked in on us making love the following morning at 7:00 am.

While we may have been apart for a year, it seemed much longer in terms of life's experiences. The more we talked, the less I seemed to know about her. In fact, I felt in some ways that I hardly knew her anymore. Perhaps she was thinking about me in the same way, but neither of us discussed it. That would come later.

During my year in Vietnam she had attended the University of Washington as an English Literature major. She was also an active war protester, taking part in many campus demonstrations. While she was against the war, she was also supportive of the troops there. (So many Americans struggled with this notion at the time.) I loved her even more for being open-minded about these controversial issues and coming to her own conclusions, despite the opinions of friends, family members, or the general public.

The first obvious sign of my PTSD didn't appear until the second evening at my parents' home, when my Dad turned on one of his favorite TV shows, *Mission Impossible*. While it was initially entertaining, I found the increasing intensity and violence to be overwhelming. (That's hard to fathom, by today's standards.) I quietly left the room, and my father didn't know what to think.

On the Ides of March, 1969, just two weeks after I returned home, Karen and I were married in St. Paul's Catholic Church in Yakima. My groomsmen included five of my closest friends from Woodland, and John Ogee, my Charlie Company medic friend who lived in Wenatchee, Washington.

It meant everything to me that John was there to celebrate our marriage. Sadly neither of us made the effort to maintain contact over the years. Years later in 2010, I made several attempts to locate him, but I was unsuccessful.

Karen and author in Woodland, WA. 1967

The PTSD Years

"But You Seem So Normal"

Following our skiing honeymoon in Whistler, British Columbia, we drove 2,700 miles to Fort Bragg, North Carolina, for my final six months of duty. Despite the fact that I was not airborne qualified, the Army assigned me to the 82nd Airborne Division, apparently due to my previous airborne unit assignment. With no on-post housing available, we lived in a trailer park, with an open sewer, next to a pig farm, during the sweltering summer. (Yes, there were aroma issues.) With the Chicago 7 on trial and associated riots, my unit was on call all summer, making it nearly impossible to get away on the weekends, let alone attend Woodstock. Despite these challenges, we managed to sneak away from time to time to enjoy the scenic coast of North Carolina.

My yet-to-be-diagnosed PTSD manifested itself through frequent nightmares. I would wake up bathed in sweat. Sometimes they became so violent I would unknowingly strike Karen with my flailing arms and legs. We were both worried by these continuing events, but we accepted them as fallout from combat.

Karen and I enrolled at Eastern Washington State University, where she pursued a BA in English and I went after a BA in Urban & Regional Planning. On one hand, it was stimulating to be back in the classroom, but the political science class discussions about the war were often more than I could handle. Anything but Vietnam was preferable. I survived those times by remaining silent, burying my feelings deeper and deeper. While I supported ongoing anti-war demonstrations, I wanted no active involvement whatsoever.

I was done with the war… at least I thought so.

The 1970s

A constant sense of restlessness consumed me during the decade of the 1970s that I could never seem to shake. The result was frequent job changes. We first lived in Longview, Washington, then Boise, Idaho, and later, Carson City, Nevada. I liked the jobs (and the cities) but it seemed every two years or so I just had to move on. Perhaps, at some level, the excitement of a new job in a different city took me away from issues that troubled me. As disruptive as it was to our life, Karen somehow put up with all of the relocations She prospered in her teaching career and earned a Masters Degree in English at the University of Nevada.

Through this time, I never shared anything about the war with my co-workers or friends. If it came up in conversation, I found a way to move to another subject. Even the birth of our two sons, Niles in 1973 and Nathan in 1976, and then raising our children, who created endless joy for us, did not diminish the uneasiness inside me.

The 1980s

We returned to the Seattle area in 1982, where I served as an Assistant City Manager with the City of Kent, and Karen worked as a middle school English teacher. I remained with the City for eleven years, but my turmoil began to manifest itself in different forms. For instance, I became increasingly troubled with the image of Vietnam veterans in the media. For the first time I found myself opening up about the effects of combat on troubled veterans, based on my personal experience, and defending their behavior. In several instances, well meaning people would say: "But *you* seem so normal." I struggled to respond.

It wasn't until 1984, when the Vietnam Veterans Memorial "Traveling Wall" (a half size, portable version of the monument) came to the Seattle Center that my young sons got their first glimpse into their father's war-related issues. After a few minutes in line to view the panels, I was overcome with grief and had to leave the building. They were perplexed when I tried to explain later what had happened.

An opportunity to see the actual memorial came in 1985 when we chaperoned Karen's American History class on a field trip to Washington, D.C. As the tour bus rolled up on an evening tour of the monuments, I couldn't get out of my seat for fear of breaking down in front of the students. It wasn't until two days later, when I approached The Wall on my own, that I finally came face-to-face with my fallen buddies. It was a brief visit. I was soon overcome with grief. Fifteen years of burying my feelings had only increased my anxiety. It wasn't until a couple of years later that later I read an article about PTSD, and realized my symptoms had a name.

As the decade came to a close, challenges in my family compounded my struggles with PTSD. Niles, now sixteen, was captain of his cross country team, and we couldn't have been prouder. However, unbeknownst to us, he had secretly been using alcohol and marijuana. Once confronted about his substance abuse, he ran away from home for two days. When he returned, we enrolled him in a rehabilitation program, only to have him disappear the day he was released... this time for *five and half* torturous months. We tried every way imaginable to find him, including Karen and Nathan driving the highways of central New Mexico and Texas after we received a tip from a friend. Then one evening, a highway patrolman from Springfield, Missouri called with news. They had found Niles at a rest stop. Through Greyhound's Child Runaway Program, he was sent back home at no cost.

The 1990s

The decade of the 1990s brought new challenges to our family, which further compounded my PTSD symptoms. Niles continued to battle his addiction as he went from one rehabilitation program to another. He never remained in high school long enough to graduate. It broke our hearts and strained our marriage.

We decided we wanted to escape the suburbs, so we bought a home in the Queen Anne neighborhood of Seattle, thinking somehow things would get better. They did not. As my frustrations increased, I wanted to run away from the troubles on the home front. The tipping point was my desire to escape the dark and gloomy winters of the Northwest and move to Southern California. Karen was against the idea, as we would be separated from our family and friends. Despite this, I applied for some jobs in SoCal. I was offered, and accepted, the Deputy City Manager position in Simi Valley, forty miles northwest of Los Angeles, in spring of 1993. I thought Karen would change her mind at some point, but that wasn't the case. We eventually divorced, and I have remained in Southern California since.

It was a very selfish decision on my part. I had abandoned my sons and my wife at a time when they most needed me. I regret my actions to this day, despite my sons' forgiveness.

In the years following our divorce, Niles has lived with me for a few months, and he has since called many places home. He currently resides in Colorado with his lovely wife, Lara, and he has been straight and sober for fifteen years. I fly to Seattle a few times a year to see Nathan, his wife Jenny, and their sons Sam, Eli, and Tom. Despite efforts to stay closely connected to my sons, grandsons, and family, the time we spend together is never enough. It has been a considerable price to pay, on many levels.

Here We Go Again

The vintage Land Rover climbed the steep and slippery dirt road with ease, carrying our four person tour group deep into the nineteen thousand acre Central Rainforest Reserve in St. Lucia. Pamela and I exchanged smiles as we ate fresh mangos picked by Robert, our tour guide, during a brief stop minutes earlier. We were excited about hiking the Enbas Saut, at the bottom of Falls Trail, and chatted about it with the couple from Chicago sitting next to us.

When we reached the end of the primitive road, we were greeted by Pierre, a park ranger. He explained our hike would first take us down the mountain about a thousand vertical feet to see the falls, and then back up the other side of the valley.

The air was saturated from a brief downpour that ended just as we arrived at the trailhead. As we made our way along the path with the ranger in the lead and me in the rear, the sun broke through the dark clouds, reflecting thousands of water droplets falling from the jungle canopy above us. They sparkled and created a dazzling sight.

Stepping as quietly as possible, Pamela and I picked our way around the puddles and over the rocks while listening to hear the call of the brilliantly colored and illusive St. Lucia Parrot. After hiking for half an hour, we still had yet to hear or see one of the magnificent birds, but we were content to simply enjoy the tropical tranquility of the Reserve.

Pierre led us to an opening in the jungle where he pointed in an easterly direction to Mt. Gimie, the highest point on the island. The landform was distinctive, with steep slopes, dense underbrush and an angular flat top. As I peered across the valley at the mist-shrouded peak, it looked strangely familiar—perhaps too familiar. It was identical to the mountain where I endured my first day of combat. Three guys I rode out with on the chopper that morning were all killed by noon. Later that day, Navy Phantom jets mistakenly fired us up, killing four more and wounding twice as many. Memories of the sight and smell of brains trickling out of my buddy's skull, agonizing screams from the wounded, and the insanity of it all began flooding through my head.

I was suffocating.

It was a day I had tried to forget for the past thirty-five years, and here it was, like a boomerang nightmare… returning on my honeymoon to mess with me once again.

I turned my back to the mountain, searching for a distraction to erase the images from my mind. Heliconia flowers came into view. The black and orange petals were stunning against the backdrop of dark green foliage. Grabbing my camera, I focused on the flowers and took a couple of shots, paused and took three more. Relaxing a bit, I knelt down, traced the petals with my right forefinger and sniffed the air trying to detect a slight scent. The symmetrical tiered structure of the plant seemed to defy gravity, and I intentionally lingered a few moments longer taking it all in. *There, much better, I can breathe again…*

Turning, I realized everyone was well down the trail, and I needed to pick up the pace. With each step I wondered—just what the hell was going on in my head? Here I was, enjoying every moment of the day with my new wife, and this shit had to come into mind, triggered by *one* brief look at Mt. Gimie. Or was it a combination of factors?

Thinking back, I realized the last time I had been in a jungle was when I stayed on the North Shore of Oahu on a solo trip in 2001. I took the old Likelike Highway between Honolulu and Kaneohe to explore part of the undeveloped Kollau Range. After a mile or so, I started to get a strange creepy sensation. I had no idea what it was, but decided to return to the main road and head down to the beach. The feeling was gone before I knew it and I never gave it another thought.

Now, that same haunting sensation had returned. On a logical level, I knew it was a flashback. I had experienced a number of them over the years. Usually I was able to manage my emotions. But the feeling this time was so powerful, that it caught me by surprise. I forced myself to think about why I was here trying to clear my head. *It's 2003 and you're in peaceful St. Lucia… you're on your honeymoon…*

It didn't work.

The sunlight filtering through the jungle canopy above was dimming. It felt like everything was starting to close in. I sensed someone was following me. My muscles were tensing up throughout my entire body.

"Are you OK? You look like you are in pain," Pamela said, as I caught up to her.

"It's just some Vietnam stuff. Not to worry. It will go away. It always does," I responded.

"Well, just let me know if I can help. I love you!" Pamela said, as she gave me a hug. "Isn't it just beautiful here?" she added.

We continued descending deeper into the valley and soon the canopy was so thick the sun was completely obscured. My stomach tightened. The vines dangling above my head resembled slithering giant pythons, ready to drop down and wrap themselves around my neck, squeezing the life out of me.

Someone *was* behind me. I *knew* it. I had to protect my platoon's rear flank. I pivoted around and scanned the jungle for movement. My senses were on high alert. Did I just hear something move out there? I know I did. Where's the sound coming from?

"Jim, what are you doing? What's going on? Are you okay?" Pamela asked.

"I think a guy is back there... following us," I said in a whisper as I turned halfway around to face her.

"If someone is behind us, he's probably just another park ranger," Pamela said in a reassuring tone.

"I'm sorry... I just can't seem to shake this goddamn flashback. It started when we looked at the mountain. It took me right back to the goddamn war, my first day in combat. It was one of my worst days of my tour. I know I must sound really weird. Maybe you think I'm crazy. I've been trying to talk myself out of it, but..."

"Why don't you walk in front of me? Would that help?" Pamela offered.

I nodded, passed her, and began looking into the palm trees for one of the parrots. There had to be one somewhere out there. *If I could just focus on spotting one of those birds... maybe get a photograph.* That would allow me to refocus.

A few minutes later, the guy from Chicago, just ahead of me, began using his walking stick to strike everything within his reach. He hit tree trunks, branches, vines, and rocks. WHACK, WHACK, WHACK, WHACK...

It was fucking annoying. It wasn't just the sound reverberating in my ears; it was the fact that he was even *doing it* in the first place. This was a damn nature trail. We were there to enjoy the quiet beauty of the Reserve, be one with nature—all that sort of thing—not to put up with some dumb shit beating the hell out of every living thing in his path.

What in God's name was he thinking? I was trying to hear the call of the St. Lucia Parrot and he was scaring away every creature within a mile!

I had visions of Private Youngblood always making unnecessary and irritating noise when we were pulling an ambush... putting all of Charlie Company at risk. He was also the one who set off our trip flares in the night, fell asleep on guard and always left the safety off his M16. He nearly got us killed several times he was so fucking inept. This guy was

Youngblood's twin. I wanted to grab his stick and beat him to a pulp. *Take that, shit-for-brains!*

It was fucking 1968 all over again. Happy honeymoon.

The Wall, April 27, 2004

Slumped against the Vietnam Memorial, sobs wracked my body. I had just placed my palm on panel W 49, soldiers lost during 1968-1969. The names of forty-nine members of Charlie Company, 2nd/501st Infantry, 101st Airborne Division, etched in white against the polished ebony granite, were everywhere. As I found each one, I ran my fingers from left to right over one letter at a time.

> TOMMY BREHM   RICHARD DUNLAP
> JAMES FOSTER   RAMOS LOPEZ

Grief possessed me with such force I crumbled to my knees. When I was able to speak to Pamela, emotions buried, for decades, erupted with volcanic force followed by an unthinkable confession.

"I fucking killed her. I shot a twelve-year old girl when she wouldn't stop running away," I heard myself say again and again.

On one level I knew they were *my* words, but on another, I had no conscious knowledge of this tragic event. What girl? I never shot a child. This did not happen. Wouldn't I have remembered such a horrid event?

Distraught and confused, I went on crying, the words spewing forth despite Pamela's attempts to console me. My first day in combat… a sniper killing my best buddy… torturing and shooting prisoners… threatening to kill Private Youngblood… jungle rot… my mental breakdown…

An hour later, exhausted, I rested my body against the panel. Pamela's hand patted my shoulder. The soothing coolness of the stone permeated the back of my neck. Closing my eyes, I took slow, deliberate breaths and absorbed the energy of The Wall. The collective spirit of the fallen soldiers took me wherever it wanted. As the minutes passed, the reality of what happened thirty-six years earlier began to materialize.

The scene unfolded as if I was viewing it from a distant perch through a camera's telescopic lens. With each twist of the zoom more detail was revealed.

The wide-angle view encompassed the expansive terrain between the Thien Thu Mountains to the west and the South China Sea to the east. Here, rice paddies, palm groves and small villages dominate the landscape. A few turns of the zoom lens brought several thatched roof structures into view. I could see second platoon approaching. Two young women began sprinting across a rice paddy.

Looking closer I saw a soldier aiming an M16 at them. The rifle fired. One of the girls dropped to the ground. Villagers rushed to her aid.

Now the shooter filled the entire field of view with a final twist of the lens. He looked in my direction, grasped the front lip of his helmet, and tugged it down in a nod of recognition.

I recoiled as I realized… the young soldier was me.

Pamela and author at The Wall, April, 2004 (Washington Post)

Steve

"When are you planning to see a therapist?" Pamela asked with a mixture of concern and anger in her voice. "I hate to keep bringing this up, but you promised me on the plane ride home from D.C. last year that you would see one," she added.

"You're right, you're right. It's just that I'm not sure where to start. Hell, I've never seen a therapist. The idea of talking about my war experiences is really uncomfortable," I replied.

"Well, I made a call the other day to Steve Magit, a counselor in Santa Monica that a friend of mine raved about. It turns out he's a Vietnam vet as well. I gave him an overview of our situation and he would like to meet with the two of us," she said.

Two weeks later we were sitting in Steve's office. After I answered a few questions, he responded with a description of typical PTSD symptoms. They all sounded so familiar. He suggested I schedule a follow up appointment with him.

"I will do it, but first I want to give it some additional thought," I said.

"What if I provided counseling at no cost?" Steve countered.

"That's a very generous gesture. Do you really mean it?" I said.

"Yes. I provide gratis work from time to time as part of my practice. So, can I put you down for 1:00 pm next Thursday?" Steve said.

The following week I was back in his office listening to his thoughts on how we would proceed.

"What you really need to do is start writing about your war experiences, especially the bad stuff," Steve said. "The more you write about things that haunt you, the better you will feel. A good starting point might be your first day in combat. I imagine that will be tough. If that's too difficult, you can always begin with lighter topics and work your way into the more challenging situations. Trust me, it will work."

With that, Steve and I met weekly, for nine months. I began the writing exercise once I found my Little Red Notebook. I would read one of my daily cryptic passages and then write a page or two about the experience. Some were much more troublesome than others, so I would skip to the next one. On a day when I felt stronger, I went back to those

I had set aside, and continued on. I was determined to get through even the most painful memories because I had faith in Steve's methodology.

Over the next few months I found that the more I wrote, the easier it became. When I read the passages to Steve, the words flowed freely, describing events that in some cases I had put out of my mind for decades. As I worked my way through each issue, I was relieved to get so much weight off of my chest. Over time my anxiety about my war experience began to decline ever so slowly. I even noticed a slight reduction in my combat-fueled nightmares.

At the end of our last session in June of 2007, Steve said, "You should consider writing a memoir. Not only will you continue to benefit from the exercise, there might be some vets out there who will better understand their PTSD issues from reading about yours."

"Well, I will give it some thought, but at this moment I'm not so sure," I responded as I stood up to leave.

"Steve, I can't thank you enough for everything you have done for me," I said with tears welling up in my eyes. You have given me a path to follow that I know will provide me with some peace of mind… at long last." Giving him a hug, I headed for the door.

Just before I left he said, "It was the least I could do after what you have been through. Let's stay in touch."

A few months later I enrolled in a UCLA creative nonfiction class and began writing as Steve had suggested, which eventually became this memoir. It was something I would continue to do for the next eight years.

Going Back, 2009

Equatorial Hotel

The sweet aroma of Vietnamese cigarette smoke caught my attention as the aging elevator door creaked open. It was 6:45 a.m. on our first morning in Ho Chi Minh City. Pamela was still sleeping up in our room as I walked across the vintage lobby. Inhaling deeply through my nose, the familiar scent was comforting for some reason. Looking around the large room, I felt as if I had just stepped into a hotel lobby in "The Quiet American," a Michael Caine film about French Indochina in the early 1950's.

A young Vietnamese bellhop, dressed in classic attire to complement the Art Deco theme, greeted me in perfect English. He pushed open the front door and said, "Good morning, sir. I wish you a wonderful day."

"Thank you, and I hope you have one as well," I replied as I stepped through the threshold.

Before I reached the white marble veranda overlooking Tran Binh Trong Street, the sound of a hundred motorcycles and scooters with their horns blaring filled my head. The scent of cigarettes from the hotel was replaced by the combination of exhaust fumes, smoke from outdoor stoves and decaying tropical vegetation. I stood frozen in place, gazing up and down the street, taking everything in. It seemed this part of old Saigon hadn't changed a bit.

A year earlier, to commemorate the fortieth anniversary of my return from the war, I decided it was time to go back. Pamela agreed after we kicked around the idea for a few weeks. We signed up for a twelve-day tour with Gate 1 Travel. This was not specifically for vets. I didn't need any additional drama. There were thirty tourists, mostly from the San Francisco area. The itinerary included five stops from Ho Chi Minh City to Hanoi, with stays in between including Hoi An, Hue, (where I saw the most combat) and Halong Bay.

My intent was to see the new Vietnam firsthand and experience what my counselor Steve called "replacement memory." In other words, return to the source of my war memories and replace them with contemporary images of this rapidly progressing Third World country. I knew it would be difficult, but I was up for the challenge. After decades of PTSD, I would try anything for more peace of mind.

For Pamela it was an opportunity to visit Southeast Asia for the first time and capture the images on her new digital camera. And she was there to support me if things didn't go well. As it turned out, most of the tour went better than expected, but I did suffer a major setback on the first day at the War Remnants Museum.

War Remnants Museum

I slumped against the gigantic track of the American M-48A3 Patton tank parked on the north side of the museum compound. The heavy green steel armor was already hot, despite the fact it was only mid-morning on a hazy January day. The heat from the tank penetrated my blue jeans and the back of my shirt as I adjusted my posture in a futile attempt to find a comfortable position. A pool of sweat formed and ran down the middle of my back. Stopping here was no use.

Walking around the mammoth tank, I searched for a quiet shady spot to cool off and get a grip on my growing anxiety. I was angry with myself because I couldn't even make it through the first of five exhibits at the War Remnants Museum in Ho Chi Minh City. The enlarged black and white photos graphically illustrating the human toll taken during the 124-year French occupation of Vietnam were too much for me to handle.

I spotted an empty bench and picked up my stride in hopes of having it to myself. Sitting down, I held my head in my hands and began sobbing. Soon I was hyperventilating. I tried to take slow measured breaths as I massaged my temples. *Relax, man, just try and relax...*

Like an endless film loop, images of war rolled through my head, complete with smell and sound. From the earthy odor of Peterson's brains on my face after he was shot by a sniper to the eerie "pop" sound of a mortar round being launched… followed seconds later by the inevitable explosion and screams as my buddies in Charlie Company were torn apart by shrapnel. It was all there for me to relive, as it had been thousands of times before. *Why in the hell did I ever come back to this country? What in the fuck was I thinking?*

I had to walk, burn some energy. Jumping to my feet, I began moving around the far side of the exhibit yard and found myself surrounded by several U.S. military aircraft. It was as if they were staring at me.

Off to the left, I saw a F-5A fighter jet and thought of how many times the Navy pilots came to our rescue, spraying the enemy with twenty-millimeter cannon fire and dropping their lethal payloads. How surreal it was to see them now. The once highly functional and proud aircraft sat there like enormous metal tombstones in a graveyard, now a reminder to visitors that the United States had indeed lost the war. Yes, along with all of the other crap that was piled on Vietnam vets, we had the dubious distinction of being the first to lose an American war. It doesn't get any better than that.

I changed direction again, feeling anxious, and looked for a way out of the compound. Fixated on what appeared to be an exit gate in the distance, I nearly tripped over several decommissioned five hundred pound bombs on display, including the notorious BIU-82, or "Daisy Cutter." Weighing 15,000 pounds, the Smart Car-sized bombs could obliterate everything within a thousand feet. I stood my ground and stared down the monster. Christ, if anything epitomized both the strength and futility of America's firepower, it was this weapon. We had all of the technology imaginable, but it proved to be useless against an enemy that was willing to sacrifice anything and everything to win.

Like a steel ball bouncing around the inside of a vintage pinball machine, I walked back and forth across the compound. Eventually I returned to the bench to wait for Pamela, who had gone on to view the other exhibits. Focusing on the weeds between cobblestones, I tried to regain my composure. It was just a small setback. *Things will be fine. You can make it through this place.*

Letting out a huge sigh, my eyes were drawn to the large Communist flag flying proudly above the museum. The morning breeze fluttered the bright red cloth with its contrasting yellow star. I gazed at the flag, unable to take my eyes away. How could this iconic symbol of North Vietnam's victory over the United States look so peaceful and serene? I came here thinking that seeing the flag might fill me with resentment and anger. Instead, the undulating fabric just looked surreal.

I stood up and looked out towards Ho Chi Minh City's central business district. I could see everything had changed—from the towering office buildings, to the name of the city. The Vietnamese had moved on. The "American War" (as they called it) was the furthest thing from these peoples' minds. But my head was still forty years in the past.

Across the exhibit yard I saw a dusty green H-1 Huey helicopter, perhaps thirty feet away. For me, these birds were the most enduring image of the war. They were our lifeline. After taking us into combat, Hueys brought food and mail to keep us going, and came to our rescue when we were in deep shit.

As I studied the scars on the nose of the chopper, my mind began to drift. I could hear the rising whine of the turbine engine, feel the wind on my face as the rotor blades began to churn, and knew the pungent smell of death would soon follow.

Get a grip, man, get a grip. Get your head out of the fucking past.

Walking back to the tour bus, I did my best to ignore members of our tour. I didn't need any conversation right now. Putting one foot in front of another in a measured stride, I reached the open door in a couple of minutes. The chilled air inside was soothing as I made my way to my seat. The cocooned environment of the bus removed me from the realties outside. Just what I needed.

Closing my eyes, I rubbed my temples, trying to relax while I waited for Pamela and the rest of the group to return.

Things will get better from here on, man. At least you gave the museum a try.

Reunification Palace (site of end of Vietnam War) January, 2009

Roses on the Song Bo

Following a couple of relaxing days in beautiful Hoi An, a fishing village (and World Heritage Site) on the Thu Bon River where it meets the South China Sea, our tour bus made its way north up the central coast towards Da Nang on Highway One. It's a mostly paved two-lane road, over a thousand miles long, connecting Ho Chi Minh City with Hanoi. We chatted with our fellow travelers about how much we loved the array of historic buildings in Hoi An, all somehow untouched by the war. For the first time since our arrival, it felt comfortable to be back in Vietnam. I was starting to feel like a regular tourist.

Just south of the city where Highway One hugs the coast, the driver pulled over when we reached China Beach. It had been a popular R&R center during the war that I had never seen. The undeveloped sugar white sand stretched north and south for miles. It was a sunny eighty-degree day with a light breeze. Perfect head high sets rolled into the shore, with not a surfer in sight. In fact, the beach was void of people, an unimaginable scene back home in Southern California.

Walking up the beach hand in hand, Pamela asked me, "How are you feeling?"

"Better and better. I am overwhelmed at times with the magnitude of change. But I try to focus on the beauty of this country, like this bay. It's so unspoiled. I never would have imagined. And to be here with you makes it that much more special. I can't thank you enough for your support each day. I love you more than ever," I said.

After driving through Da Nang (were I spent a month in the 95th Evac Hospital in 1968), the bus lumbered up scenic Hai Van Pass. We took in the dramatic views of the South China before heading north towards Hue.

For the next hour or more, while Pamela napped, I sat quietly staring out the bus window, looking for remnants of the war, and seeing nothing. The people and the countryside had recovered. The war-torn Vietnam in my mind was a memory of what *once was*. I still needed to make the transition from the past to present. It was a process. This was just the first step.

As the bus passed the twenty-five kilometer road sign to Hue, my mind drifted back to the last time I was on this highway in March, 1968.

Moments after landing at Phu Bai airstrip, we were herded on to open air "deuce and a half" trucks. From there, my group of perhaps eighty soldiers made our way in an unarmed convoy to Hue, still smoldering from the month-long Tet Offensive that had just ended. The air had a curious mixture of aromas. Along with the burning wood and oil, I smelled decaying tropical vegetation and rotting flesh from a few dead water buffalos in the ditch next to the road. Were human bodies from the 6,000 civilians killed during the fighting in Hue in the ditch as well? I wasn't sure, but the thought of it fueled my rising anxiety.

Without any weapons, we couldn't have been more vulnerable, sitting high up on the truck benches as civilians below begged us for cigarettes and Cokes. ARVAN soldiers waved and smiled as we passed by. And GIs taunted us with jeers, "fucking cherries" being the most popular. We were wide-eyed and scared shitless.

Letting out a big sigh, I shifted my attention back to the Lonely Planet guide to Vietnam in my lap and read the following passage.

"Hue, with a population of 250,000, is the most beautiful city in all of Vietnam and served as the political capital from 1802 to 1945. The most notable feature is the Citadel, a fortress built in 1864 protected by a six-mile long, 30-foot high stone wall complete with a moat. Erected in the early 19th century, the Old Imperial City (inside the fortress) was modeled after the Forbidden Beijing, and is home to a wealth of palaces and temples."

Sadly, the Citadel became "ground zero" during the Tet Offensive in 1968 because the Communist forces used it as their headquarters. The structure suffered hits by small arms fire and rockets. Thankfully, the U.S. held back on bombing the Citadel, respecting the history of the structure. I recalled seeing damage to the massive walls as our convoy passed the main gate, but the fortress looked impressive just the same.

Our room at the Century Riverside Hotel had an expansive deck overlooking the Song Huong (Perfume River). While Pamela's eyes were focused on the boats drifting by, mine were drawn to the mountains east of the city. A distinctive ridgeline, highlighted in the late day sun, caught my attention and my stomach knotted up.

"What's wrong?" Pamela said, as she watched me recoil and sit down on a lounge chair.

"See those mountains out there? That's where I spent most of my tour when I wasn't in the lowlands. The ridge most further to the left is where I survived my first day in combat. Three of the guys I rode out with in a Huey that morning died before the end of the day. I just can't believe I'm here in this beautiful hotel looking at what was once Hell," I said, shaking my head.

The following day we had several hours to ourselves. I had two objectives. Find the location of what was once Camp Sally and then visit the Song Bo River to pay tribute to my fallen brothers. Both locations were several kilometers north on Highway One.

Finding Sally, with the help of a taxi driver who couldn't speak any English, turned out to be an adventure in itself. It was made even more difficult because the countryside had transformed in forty years from pastoral to suburban. The landscape was unrecognizable to me. Using an old military map I found online and a few landmarks, we eventually located the former Camp Sally site. It was now a modern cement plant, of all things. The irony created a needed moment of levity for the two of us.

Reaching the bridge where the highway crossed the Song Bo was much easier. My brief memorial ceremony was not. Walking out on the bridge with a bouquet of yellow roses, I stopped mid-span and gazed up the river towards the mountains to the east. Aside from the noise of traffic behind me, it was a tranquil day. The mountains were carpeted with an uninterrupted layer of Kelly green jungle. Such a contrast to pocks of brown created by American bombs and Agent Orange drops during the war. Their original beauty had been fully restored and I savored the sight for a moment or two.

Despite the peaceful scene, images began flooding my mind as I remembered how each one of my buddies lost their lives four decades earlier: ambushes, booby traps, firefights, snipers, and even a drowning.

And for what? I sensed I would never be able to shake my deep resentment toward everything about this war.

One by one, I dropped each rose into the Song Bo in their memory. Saying a brief prayer for their souls, I also thanked God for giving me the gift of life.

When I walked back to Pamela, she gave me a huge hug. Tears filled her eyes. She said, "You are the strongest man I know."

"I don't know about that. It was the least I could do for my guys. They gave everything… and we still lost the war," I replied. "It is just a fucking shame."

Author at Perfume River Bridge, July, 1968

Author at Perfume River Bridge, January, 2009

Celebrating Tet

Visiting Vietnam in January was timely in a couple of ways. First, it was the dry season, with low humidity and moderate temperatures. Second, it coincided with the annual celebration of Tet. That gave us an opportunity to witness Vietnamese enjoying their favorite time of year from Ho Chi Minh City to Hanoi. I viewed that as a bonus in my quest to replace bad memories with new ones. My only experience with the holiday period previously was the horrific Tet Offensive of 1968.

Tet is the traditional Vietnamese New Year and comes some time between late January and March. Its name is the shortened version of *tet nguyen dan* (first morning of the new period). This is the time to forgive and forget, and to pay off debts. It is also everyone's birthday. The Vietnamese tend not to celebrate their birthdays, but everyone adds one year to their age at Tet.

Great attention is paid to preparations for Tet because the first week of the New Year is believed to dictate your fortunes for the year to come. Enormous quantities of goods are consumed, houses are painted, and new clothes are bought, especially red outfits for toddlers.

We found evidence of Tet everywhere when we first arrived, from red and gold decorations throughout the airport, to banners draped across major streets and even the lobby of our hotel. Perhaps the most dramatic images, however, were bright yellow kumquat trees strapped to the back of motorbikes that zipped by, headed to homes for good luck and prosperity.

The presence of Tet increased with each city we visited, culminating with New Year's Eve in Hanoi. Peering out of the sixteenth floor of our Sofitel hotel room, just before midnight, we watched decorative paper lanterns powered by candle heat rise above thousands of people on the street below. It was a scene like no other.

"This is so magical," Pamela said. "What could be more symbolic of your new buoyancy than these colorful lanterns floating skyward?"

"Indeed… indeed," I replied.

As the eleventh and final day of our Vietnam adventure came to a close, I realized the visit had given me more peace of mind than I ever could have imagined. I had accomplished my goals, thanks to the constant support of my amazing wife every step of the way.

Pamela and Author, Halong Bay, January, 2009

MAKING PEACE WITH IT ALL

Panel W 49, May 30, 2013

Returning to The Wall was something I had anticipated since March when I learned my employer, U.S. VETS, had scheduled a groundbreaking event for a new homeless veterans shelter in Washington D.C. It would be my first opportunity to visit the Vietnam Memorial in nine years.

I was on edge and alone by choice. Would I have an emotional meltdown like the last time? Or, would I keep my feelings under control? I couldn't be sure, and I didn't want to make a scene.

Climbing out of a cab at 6:45 a.m., I saw American flags by the thousands lining the pathway towards The Wall. Placed there during the Memorial Day celebration three days earlier, they were motionless in the warm and humid air.

Squinting into the rising sun, I surveyed the entire five hundred-foot length of the charcoal colored granite structure in the distance. Not a person in sight. I had the place all to myself. Perfect.

I took slow deliberate steps, admiring the simplistic design. Cut into the landscape, the height of the first seventy panels increased proportionally with the decrease in the path elevation. After walking down a short distance, the names of the dead rose from my ankle to my waist. By the time I reached the apex of the memorial, the names loomed four feet above my head.

As I gazed at the stone surface, I saw my reflection in the polished marble. Dressed in black Nike running shorts and a white t-shirt, my image was distinct and yet enveloped by hundreds of names, depending on how I focused my eyes. Minutes passed as I stood there without a single distraction. The longer I remained, the more I felt connected to my fallen brothers. On one level, it was soothing and comforting. Closing my eyes, I relaxed and let the sensation consume me.

But as time passed, I began feeling uneasy. Tension was building up inside my body. It was as if the names, extending to my left, right and above me, had weight and were pressing down on me. Despite the discomfort, I was determined not to leave. I was here to prove to myself that I was stronger now, and that I was able to put my tragic memories into a healthier perspective.

Sitting down on the stone walkway, I looked east towards the Washington Monument. It was covered in scaffolding to repair the earthquake damage from the year earlier. The distraction was just enough for me to keep my emotions in check and I began to feel less anxious. *You're okay, man. Just hang in there. It's all part of the experience. There is nothing to fear. You are in control.*

After some time, I collected myself and rose to my feet. As I made my way to panel W 49, I saw a range of items, from teddy bears, flowers and flags, to small notes, letters, and poems placed at the base of The Wall. All were tributes to the dead from family, friends, and admirers. One poem outlined in red, white, and blue stars caught my eye, and I knelt down to read it.

Soldiers
by Morgan Peters

For the lives lay down to save our home,
For the bravery and strength that you've shown,
For the many memories that left painful scars,
For committing to your duty with all of your heart,
For being a hero and leader to us all,
For fighting in battle and standing up tall,
For pushing through in the darkest of times,
For all of the family you've had to leave behind,
For the days when you feel like you can't take any more,
For the years that you've spent with the burden of war,
For the faces of friends and loved ones you've lost,
For protecting our country no matter the cost,
For pride in our country that you've proved to the world,
For the mothers and fathers and boys and girls,
For the love in our hearts we stand here today,
Thank you to our veterans and God bless the USA.

Building on my growing confidence, I scanned W 49 to find some of my buddies, something that undid me nine years ago. Once I found a few names, I ran my fingers from left to right one letter a time.

    GEORGE DORCHAK   ROBERT MOSLEY
    DONALD PURDUE   FRED FRAPPIEA

Closing my eyes, I tried to listen for their voices. Whether it was my imagination or not, it didn't matter, but I was certain after a while I could hear them calling out.

Hansen, you worthless motherfucker, you came back. We never thought we would ever fucking see you again after your meltdown. You didn't fucking forget us. You can make a difference, man. Do something, fucking anything, so people will always remember how fucked up war is. Make us count for something!

Kneeling down before W 49, I wanted to pay tribute to them and make amends with myself. Bowing my head in respect, I began reading from a note I had written earlier.

"Guys, I am here to honor each one of you and make peace with the past," I said, in a soft voice. "I deeply respect all of you for giving your lives for our country. To think that over 58,000 Americans died in the end… and, other than this humble monument, we have little to show for it. For the last forty years, I hated our nation's leaders for allowing this to happen."

Continuing on, I said, "This affected every aspect of my life… from my marriage, to the way I raised my sons, to what I have accomplished over the years. And all the way the peace of mind I was seeking was never within reach. When I returned home after my last visit here in 2004, I began seeing a therapist. He got me to realize that I had to let my resentment go. I now understand I shouldn't feel guilty for serving in the war and surviving while you did not. I had only done what my country had asked me to do. I needed to refocus my feelings. It has been a long process but I am ever closer to my goal."

"I wouldn't be alive today had it not been for all of you covering my back," I said. "Thank you all from the bottom of my heart for your dedication and conviction to the men of Charlie Company, 2/501st Infantry, 101st Airborne. God bless you."

Standing up, I saluted The Wall and once again saw my image reflecting in the black marble. Minutes passed as I stood at attention and thought about the war, my forty-nine lost buddies and many more who were wounded. While I felt a deep sense of sorrow, it was offset by a sense of reconciliation.

I turned and walked back up the incline to the very bench where I had sat with my wife, Pamela, years before. In the distance, I could see the monument sparkling in the morning sun. A smile came across my face as I realized peace of mind was at hand. I was a different man now and ready to move forward in my life. The horror of the war would no longer define me. From this point on, it would instead provide me with a deep sense of appreciation for life and a new sense of purpose.

What more could an old grunt like me ask for?

WHAT WORKED FOR ME MIGHT WORK FOR YOU

Ten Steps to Consider

Once I discovered the four ingredients to my PTSD (sorrow, regret, shame and guilt) I needed ways to find and stay on the path to recovery. There's nothing groundbreaking here in the field of PTSD research, but these ten steps worked for me.

1. **Find your "Mother Ocean"**
   In the early 1950s, my family built a cabin on the Long Beach Peninsula in Washington. It was situated on twenty-six miles of pristine beach. The pounding surf delivered driftwood of all kinds, from which my sisters and I constructed elaborate "forts." Predawn beachcombing after winter storms rewarded us with Japanese glass balls entwined in fishing nets, sand dollars, and seashells. There was an endless supply of Dungeness crab, Olympic oysters, and butter clams, which we even ate for breakfast. But when we were away, the thing I missed the most above all else was the salt air. I yearned for the euphoric sensation it created when I took a deep breath through my nostrils.

   Instant peace of mind.

   After the war, I rediscovered the effect salt air had on me when Karen and I visited the Cape Hatteras National Seashore while I was stationed at Fort Bragg, North Carolina, with the

82nd Airborne Division. It proved to be a natural relief from my PTSD symptoms. So it's no surprise after I left the Army that I have lived most of my adult life on or near the coast.

My infatuation with the ocean drew me to the singer, songwriter, and author Jimmy Buffet in my mid-twenties. I have been a Parrot Head (as his devout fans are called) ever since. His music celebrates the magic of the tropics and I have used it to maintain a connection to the ocean, especially while living elsewhere. One of my favorites is entitled "Mother Ocean." The lyrics capture that special feeling. By turning up the volume and closing my eyes, I can channel all of those soothing sensations.

So, what is your "Mother Ocean?" If you don't have one, then maybe you need to start looking.

2. **Reach out to family and friends for support**

This may seem obvious, but while I was blessed with a solid family network and wonderful friends to come home to after the war, I didn't look to them for support. For decades, I thought I could manage my PTSD on my own. I was convinced if someone hadn't served in combat, they would never understand. Yet by silently internalizing my feelings, I compounded my condition.

When I did finally reach out a few years ago to family and friends, a flood of love and support followed. It was just so easy. Whatever was I thinking?

3. **Embrace your veteran status**

Like so many Vietnam vets, I was embarrassed to have served in the first war the United States ever lost. I was ashamed to have killed Vietnamese, burned their villages, and destroyed their countryside. I felt the war was one of America's greatest mistakes. I rarely told anyone that I had served, and went so far as to never put my military service on my resume. In fact, I didn't seek out any veteran services or benefits beyond my GI

Bill to pay for college. I wanted to remain as distant as possible from all things military.

With the vast array of benefits available from the Veterans Administration (VA) and assistance from nonprofits such as U.S. VETS, AmVets, Goodwill and others, and generous corporate donors like The Home Depot, the resources seem endless. If you have a need today, someone is there to help. But you will have to do your homework and be assertive, especially with the VA. For every wonderful benefit and program, plan on filling out multiple applications. Patience is required.

In 2011, Mike Murray, a good friend and a fellow Vietnam combat veteran, encouraged me to join the U.S. VETS Advisory Council in Long Beach. U.S. VETS is the nation's largest non-profit serving homeless veterans. It was the first time in four decades I had been around veterans, and I loved the experience. Our common bond gave me renewed strength and a sense of belonging. Less than a year later, I was appointed Executive Director of their facility in Long Beach, housing 550 veterans each night. It was crazy busy, very challenging, but so satisfying at the end of each day. I was giving back to vets on many levels, easing the sense of guilt I had carried for years for turning my back on them. The high point for me was being the featured speaker at the 50th Annual Memorial Day Celebration at Forest Lawn Cemetery in 2014. It was the first time I ever opened up publicly about my combat experience I described my PTSD and measures I have taken to come to terms with my demons. The response from the 600 attendees was overwhelming and I reveled in their support.

4. **Write down what haunts you (and burn it in your fireplace)**
When you are feeling anger, anxiety, frustration, or restlessness, write down each issue on separate pieces of paper. Once you have listed them all, wad each one up and toss them in the fireplace. (I credit my counselor Steve with this idea.) Pamela and I do this

every New Year's Eve and we encourage our party guests to do the same. The purpose is to unload the negativity in your life. It is an uplifting exercise that takes the emotional weight from your shoulders and provides a refreshing start to the New Year.

Without consciously knowing it, I found a way to "write out" my feelings during the war by keeping both a daily diary in The Little Red Notebook and my 224 letters to home. At the end of each day, I put pen to paper, describing my experiences and venting as needed. I am convinced it helped me to maintain my emotional balance, especially during some of the worst stages of the war.

5. **Seek out a qualified therapist and/or veteran support group**
I first realized combat had lingering effects on the day I returned home from the war, February 27, 1969. My father turned on one of his favorite TV shows, *Mission Impossible* and I had to leave the living room because of the violence. I was angry with myself and embarrassed for my behavior. Also, the distant sound of chopper blades, especially from Hueys or Chinooks, was unnerving, and I couldn't run from it. Horrific images of medivak rescues and combat air assaults consumed me every time one flew overhead. But it was the frequent nightmares about combat I dreaded the most. I would thrash about in bed sometimes, injuring my former wife and breaking into night sweats.

While some of these PTSD symptoms decreased over the next thirty years, I found others, such as nightmares and auditory triggers, increasing in frequency in the late 1990s. I was clueless as to why. All of this came to head in 2004 when I visited The Wall. My meltdown was a first for me. I had never lost complete control of myself in my entire civilian life. Pamela and I both agreed I needed some help. Finally, when I returned home to Southern California, I began seeing a counselor.

To our surprise, that meltdown at The Wall was captured from a distance by a *Washington Post* photographer and a reporter doing a story on Senator John Kerry's campaign for President.

They both approached me apologetically and asked if I would agree to an interview. Once I composed myself, I was asked to comment on Senator Kerry's military experience that had been called into question by his opposition. I responded the Senator's experience was an asset because he served his country in a war zone and experienced combat. Whether he deserved the medals was irrelevant. The *Post* ran the story on the following day.

(See cover photo and page 136.)

6. **Challenge your sense of helplessness by assisting veterans and others who are in need**

    Veteran service organizations are always looking for volunteers. At U.S. VETS in Long Beach, we were blessed to have a number of individuals and service organizations assist our veterans on a regular basis. Activities ranged from events like the Huntington Beach Elks Club annual BBQ to contributions of clothing and food from caring nearby residents.

    No matter the activity or gesture, volunteers typically walk away feeling a sense of satisfaction. They gain a fresh perspective on the challenges facing vets… and perhaps some insight into themselves.

7. **Address negative behavior that interferes with healing**

    At U.S. VETS, we found over forty percent of the incoming homeless vets were struggling with excessive use of alcohol or drugs. This retarded their ability to address their PSTD challenges, so their recovery often took much longer. Seeking professional treatment for substance abuse first, we found, set the stage for success.

8. **Reconnect with your faith**

    Regardless of your faith or individual spiritual beliefs, I think any vet suffering from PTSD can benefit from going down this path, to see what comfort might be found. Like so many of these ideas, you have nothing to lose.

9. **Find a way to celebrate being alive every day**

    For starters, you woke up this morning…

10. **Go back to your "battlefield"**

    On the fortieth anniversary of my homecoming from the war, I went back to Vietnam. For the longest time, I knew in my heart that returning to Vietnam was essential to my PTSD recovery efforts.

    Despite my initial reservations, the Vietnamese were warm and friendly wherever we went. For the most part there was no evidence of the "American War" (as they call it). The Vietnamese had moved on, just like they did following the 124-year French Occupation. If they could do it, why couldn't I?

    I flew back to Los Angeles with new memories of Vietnam—as a beautiful and peaceful country, filled with the warmest people imaginable. I had accomplished my goal of taking on my demons and bring home a fresh perspective.

    Tuyen, our tour guide, said it best when he saw me crying as I came out of the War Remnants Museum. Reaching up, he put his arm on my right shoulder. Patting it gently, he said:

    "It O.K., man, war over now. War over now."

Acknowledgements

Sandra Kobrin, my UCLA creative nonfiction instructor, provided expertise and encouragement to help me write so much of this memoir. Joyce Actor, my writing group leader, was especially supportive throughout the entire process.

Jan Knutson Stone, a writer from Key West, Florida who grew up in Sydney, Australia, was very helpful in providing details about Kings Cross during my R & R in 1969.

When life goes full circle, it can provide unexpected consequences and even inspiration. In 2011, I had the pleasure of being a Business Advisor (through Goldman Sachs 10,000 Small Businesses program at Long Beach City College) for Tin Vo, a restaurateur in Westminster (Little Saigon), California. We realized our paths must have crossed over forty years earlier in Hue. Charlie Company came in from the field every few weeks to guard the only remaining bridge over the Perfume River. School children crossed it every morning. No doubt Tin was one of the kids I would greet as they scampered over the bridge on their way to school. Tin's friendship gave me inspiration to continue writing when I most needed it.

From 2012 to 2014, I served as the Executive Director of U.S. VETS-Long Beach, a nationwide nonprofit providing shelter and critical services to 550 previously homeless vets. The experience of working with Vietnam War vets, and those who served in Afghanistan and Iraq, was insightful and rewarding. I am grateful to Steve Peck, President and CEO, for the unique opportunity to give back to my fellow vets. And thanks to Mike Murray, Chair of the U.S. VETS Advisory Council and member of the National Board of Directors. I feel blessed to call him a friend and appreciate his support at so many levels.

Mary Jane Hansen, my late mother, and Karen Koreski Hellend, my former wife, saved every letter I wrote home. Those combined 224 letters provided essential information, from facts and figures to my mindset during the war.

My sons, Niles and Nathan, offered their full support and encouragement throughout this entire process.

Steve Magit, my counselor, I cannot thank enough for his wisdom, guidance and for asking me to begin writing out my thoughts.

If it were not for my wife, Pamela, I would never have embarked on this journey. She was there for me every day over the eight-year project that has culminated in this book.

www.ingramcontent.com/pod-product-compliance
Lightning Source LLC
Chambersburg PA
CBHW071924290426
44110CB00013B/1465